"With her 'EastWorld' of an Iranian childhood ever present, Jazani's personal and poetic exploration of what makes us human – mortality, suffering, bodies, feelings – by way of myth and fairy stories, film and poetry situates Lacanian theory firmly in the clinic, with her rich accounts of her psychoanalytic practice."
— **Dr Anne Worthington,** *The College of Psychoanalysts, UK;*
Chair of the Centre for Freudian Analysis and Research

"In her own unique style, weaving together Lacanian theory, clinical vignette and autobiography, Jazani explores the questions of subjective structure, the body and the symptom. This takes her to less familiar territory in Lacanian psychoanalysis: the formative effects of fairy tales and the function and phenomenology of feelings, which she approaches through their role in Persian culture. The book has a momentum and sweep that takes the reader on a stimulating, illuminating and often unexpected journey, opening up new lines of thought and encouraging us to question old ones. Unlike so many Lacanian texts today, Jazani manages to bring theoretical expositions back to clinical situations and examples that readers will find both helpful and clarifying. The use of autobiographical elements gives the book a charming and surprising candour, and despite the recurring themes of mortality and pain, this is a book that is intensely alive.

Lacan, Mortality, Life and Language is unlike other books in the field in the breadth of its themes and the very individual knotting together of theory, example and autobiography. It will appeal to anyone interested in Lacanian psychoanalysis and psychoanalysis more generally, as well as to students of related fields such as literature, social studies, anthropology and the arts."
— **Darian Leader, psychoanalyst,** *author and founding member*
of the Centre for Freudian Analysis and Research

Lacan, Mortality, Life and Language

This work presents thoughts on the Lacanian subject: What are we as a speaking being? What makes us a human subject from a psychoanalytic perspective? Is it feelings and affect that make us a human? Or was it the Freudian invention of the unconscious that drew a line between human and a non-human?

What can be learnt from the subject of the unconscious in the clinic of psychoanalysis that can help us to approach the these questions? Berjanet Jazani takes examples from the psychoanalytic clinic as well as cultural references ranging from ancient Persia to London's Theatreland in order to elaborate the question of subjectivity, reality and truth from a psychoanalytic perspective. In the era of hyperreality, the agency of branding and marketing strategies has overshadowed the reality of a human being, his true nature and agency. The hyperreality of contemporary society creates in each individual a false hope of becoming a high-fidelity copy of their idols, and such a fallacy has led many to believe that this is what determines their being in a social bond. Jazani explores the question of the reality and mortality of a subject through a Lacanian prism, from the theorising of analytical subjectivity that starts with the Freudian Oedipal myth more than a century ago to the futurist aspiration to fabricate human beings according to some ideal model.

This book will be important reading for students and academics of Lacanian psychoanalysis, as well as professionals concerned with complex social problems.

Berjanet Jazani is a medical doctor and practising psychoanalyst in London, UK. She is the president of the College of Psychoanalysts, a member of the Centre for Freudian Analysis and Research and author of *Lacanian Psychoanalysis from Clinic to Culture* (Routledge, 2021).

The Lines of the Symbolic in Psychoanalysis Series
Series Editor:
Ian Parker
Manchester Psychoanalytic Matrix

Psychoanalytic clinical and theoretical work is always embedded in specific linguistic and cultural contexts and carries their traces, traces which this series attends to in its focus on multiple contradictory and antagonistic "lines of the Symbolic'. This series takes its cue from Lacan's psychoanalytic work on three registers of human experience, the Symbolic, the Imaginary and the Real, and employs this distinctive understanding of cultural, communication and embodiment to link with other traditions of cultural, clinical and theoretical practice beyond the Lacanian symbolic universe. The Lines of the Symbolic in Psychoanalysis Series provides a reflexive reworking of theoretical and practical issues, translating psychoanalytic writing from different contexts, grounding that work in the specific histories and politics that provide the conditions of possibility for its descriptions and interventions to function. The series makes connections between different cultural and disciplinary sites in which psychoanalysis operates, questioning the idea that there could be one single correct reading and application of Lacan. Its authors trace their own path, their own line through the Symbolic, situating psychoanalysis in relation to debates which intersect with Lacanian work, explicating it, extending it and challenging it.

Obscenity, Psychoanalysis and Literature
Lawrence and Joyce on Trial
William Simms

Lacan, Mortality, Life and Language
Clinical and Cultural Explorations
Berjanet Jazani

Psychoanalysis Under Nazi Occupation
The Origins, Impact and Influence of the Berlin Institute
Laura Sokolowsky

For more information about this series, please visit: *www.routledge.com*

Lacan, Mortality, Life and Language

Clinical and Cultural Explorations

Berjanet Jazani

Routledge
Taylor & Francis Group

LONDON AND NEW YORK

First published 2022
by Routledge
2 Park Square, Milton Park, Abingdon, Oxon OX14 4RN

and by Routledge
605 Third Avenue, New York, NY 10158

Routledge is an imprint of the Taylor & Francis Group, an informa business

© 2022 Berjanet Jazani

British Library Cataloguing-in-Publication Data
A catalogue record for this book is available from the British Library

Library of Congress Cataloging-in-Publication Data
Names: Jazani, Berjanet, 1980– author.
Title: Lacan, mortality, life and language : clinical and cultural explorations / Berjanet Jazani.
Description: 1 Edition. | new york : Routledge, 2022. | Series: The lines of the symbolic | Includes bibliographical references and index.
Identifiers: LCCN 2021015809 (print) | LCCN 2021015810 (ebook) | ISBN 9781032027029 (hardback) | ISBN 9781032027142 (paperback) | ISBN 9781003184799 (ebook) | ISBN 9781000442427 (adobe pdf) | ISBN 9781000442441 (epub)
Subjects: LCSH: Psychoanalysis. | Subconsciousness. | Language acquisition—Psychological aspects. | Immortality. | Other (Philosophy) | Reality—Psychological aspects. | Lacan, Jacques, 1901–1981.
Classification: LCC BF175 .J39 2022 (print) | LCC BF175 (ebook) | DDC 150.19/5—dc23
LC record available at https://lccn.loc.gov/2021015809
LC ebook record available at https://lccn.loc.gov/2021015810

ISBN: 978-1-032-02702-9 (hbk)
ISBN: 978-1-032-02714-2 (pbk)
ISBN: 978-1-003-18479-9 (ebk)

DOI: 10.4324/9781003184799

Typeset in Times New Roman
by Apex CoVantage, LLC

For Ben and only Ben

Contents

Figures

Acknowledgements

I would like to acknowledge the anxious feelings of all children on the earth, particularly those who grew up/grow up with no fairy tales – all the children of war. When I was writing this manuscript, a group of my childhood playmates were ever present in my thoughts. When I finished the first draft, one of those friends, Sara, emailed me out of the blue after 30 years of no contact. We were 12 friends and playmates living in the north of Tehran when the city was under bombardment. Those years were bitter and sweet: the bitterness of the war-inducing anxiety, and the sweetness of six summers with much play, adventures and ice-cream. The bitter reality was sweetened every single day each summer through our world of play: our "EastWorld"! We did not grow up with fairy tales. Our daily reality was coloured with red and white alarms. Our games and play happened between those alarms. That fantasy world ended when my family moved home. Since then, my sister and I spent each summer for the rest of our childhood re-creating the same games and adventures. But it was never the same again.

I pay homage to our childhood home in Qeytariyeh and to Sara, Elmira, Reza, Lida, Fati, Amir, Kaveh, Negin, Samira, Ali and to you, Bernadette. To hours and hours of wandering around the city with Ben, my fellow explorer, before, during and after the London lockdown. To the Sky I look up to whenever I can't find my home beneath my feet. You are always the same and reassuring. And, to the Earth and the new generations with their new and old fairy tales. Perhaps 2020 can index a new start for us to remember once again that we are the guardians of the Earth, our home, despite all of our variety and our differences.

A big thanks to my English editor, Ben Hooson, whose editing work and comments were an invaluable help.

A very special thanks to Khosro Fravahar and his love for Iran.

My sincere thanks to Ian Parker, Erica Burman, Anne Worthington, Simona Revelli, Darian Leader, Mary Horlock, Pat Blackett, Nigel Coombs, Loretta Monaco, Andrew Hodgkiss, Stephanie Hodgkiss, Mehrdad Seyf, Michelle Da Silva, Kenneth Theron, Michael Aminian, Vivien Burgoyne, Bernard Burgoyne, Renata Salecl, Bice Benvenuto, Nazy Naderi, Ginny Thomas, Astrid Zecena, Will Burns, Annette Lyons, Gerry Sullivan, Viviane Blanchard, Gwion Jones, Lisa Simone Jones, Anouchka Grose, Dot Grose, Laura Radu, Astrid Gessert, Pojhan

Omid Zohour, Ronak Khakban, Dorothea Schueler, Mehdi Baniasadi, Daniela Oliveira Grund, Narges Sharifzadeh, Mary Artemi, Faezeh Kazemi, Tajbanou Beklik, Nazy Kazemi, Kalli Nikolopoulou, Andreea Goloca, Michelle Willett, Julia Carne, Julie Burchill, Vincent Dachy, Bridget MacDonald, Dorothee Bonnigal-Katz, Tim Beazleigh, Alistair Black, Valentina Chiricallo, Luca Bosetti, Denis Echard, Vera Warchavchik, Sassi Jazani, Sarah Bolouri Jazani, Nina Nedelyaevy, Shahzad Naderi, Denis Nedelyaev, Mahshid Hajiani, Misagh Laghaei, Nayer Naderi, Stan Watts, Mark Elmer, Masoud Moeini, Ozra Fazel, Abbas Aghdaei, Masi Novin, Houshang Heydararabi, Abdi Rafatian, Parvin Jazani, Delaram Aghaei, Yaprak Olmez, Fatemeh Baghaei, Farzaneh Naderi, Majid Naderi, Kalpa Rao, Nahid Moeini, Cristina Lungu, Reza Gharachorloo, Sara Taheri, Zara Naderi, Jo Mcewan, Soudabeh Didaran, Ali Naderi, Gohar Behrouz, Mahnaz Moeini, Soheila Naderi, Aylar Ebrahimi, Parisa Naderi, Nemat Moeini, Afagh Rahim Kashi, Barsian Moeini and Bardia Moeini.

Series preface

We are born dead and we must learn how to live. This extraordinary compelling description of what we are as subjects of language, and injunction to trace our own singular path into the world, is at the heart of the book. What it is to be human is not to be happy – that idea which underpins positive psychology and its ideological armature would have been anathema to Freud – but to bear witness to what we are as embodied beings. If, for Freud, the aim of all life is death, the book faces that prospect, takes it seriously, explores its consequences and embeds "life" in our peculiar condition; we are, after all, not adapted to this life that we are thrown into, but always already "disadapted", out of joint, out of time with the simultaneously comforting and disturbing narratives of a supposedly natural life course, of the journey from birth to death. We live because we are unnatural, mortal, and that is why we speak and write about death, and must read and reflect on what the book tells us and shows us what psychoanalysis has to say about that.

Berjanet Jazani weaves together four threads of the Symbolic, of the chains of language which permit us to speak while also constraining what we can say. There is, first, an autobiographical narrative in which she anchors herself and provides us a compass for navigating our way through the Symbolic, a compass that draws attention to something very different in its nature because it is the compass of this singular subject, this author. The second thread is that of a distinctive cultural contextual reflection on what this Symbolic is for a subject born in Iran, and carrying with her the traces of that place into the language in which she now speaks to us. We learn something about Iran, about life and death in ancient Persia, and that enables us to grasp better how the world is mediated, represented and re-presented to us as what it is, as if that is only what it is. But there is more. Creative reinterpretation and representations of the world provide the third thread, in analysis of film, of some literature, but mainly film, and we are thereby taken into the realm of an Imaginary mediation of the Symbolic, reflecting on its Imaginary effects. This Imaginary, however, is not simple face-to-face communication, but complex intersecting vectors of what we are told is "reality", the vectors through which there is a continual ideological reshaping of what subjectivity is today, an ideological reshaping that film participates in as it provides new frames for understanding what psychoanalysis is.

And, fourth, as a narrative thread, woven into autobiography through the position of the analyst, and the culture in which we cannot but situate ourselves as we speak, and the creative representations of the world that give that culture its distinctive cultural-historical shape, there is the space of the clinic. The clinical material in the book is given peculiar depth by its resonance with the Symbolic and Imaginary conditions that are illuminated throughout the book. This space of the clinic is where the subject speaks, confronts their mortality, touches the Real of their body and really learns to live.

Psychoanalytic clinical and theoretical work circulates through multiple intersecting antagonistic symbolic universes. This series opens connections between different cultural sites in which Lacanian work has developed in distinctive ways, in forms of work that question the idea that there could be single correct reading and application. The Lines of the Symbolic in Psychoanalysis series provides a reflexive reworking of psychoanalysis that transmits Lacanian writing from around the world, steering a course between the temptations of a metalanguage and imaginary reduction, between the claim to provide a god's eye view of psychoanalysis and the idea that psychoanalysis must everywhere be the same. And the elaboration of psychoanalysis in the symbolic here grounds its theory and practice in the history and politics of the work in a variety of interventions that touch the real.

Ian Parker
Manchester Psychoanalytic Matrix

Figure 0.1 Madness, photograph by Bardia Moeini

Introduction

Some thoughts on the Lacanian subject: from Oedipal myth to poetry of knots

Reality and mortality

"What is reality?" I asked my father one day when I was a young child before starting primary school. He replied: "Whose reality?" Apparently, I had heard the word repeated in the debates at home regarding the new social changes in Iran (almost four decades ago). For years to come this new "reality" – as an uncanny experience – remained a much-discussed debate between generations. My father's response, "Whose reality?" complicated the nature of reality in my mind. It implied that "reality" was not an abstract idea carrying a universal meaning. Before hearing his answer, I had even thought of the term as a proper name referring to a real person, and I had wanted to see or be taken to where he was. The "reality" I had imagined had an independent nature and existence outside us, while my father's response indicated an entity that was to be subjectified, that could be created, fabricated, twisted or changed by each subject.

What does "reality" mean from a psychoanalytical perspective, when the mortal and sexualised body, which carries the marks of a social discourse, cannot be distinguished from the concept of subjectivity? What would reality have meant for a subject if mortality did not exist? If Freud puts sexuality at the heart of his invention of psychoanalysis, Lacan approached the nature of our being through an exploration of the question of mortality when he reworked the concept of the Freudian drive or when he reformulated the concept of jouissance based on the Freudian death drive. A "subjective reality" is not the same as a personal, cognitive interpretation of an external reality. The nature of reality for a subject is a product of the unconscious, where it is both built and perceived. In psychoanalysis, the concepts of reality and dream do not have as clear a boundary as we understand them to have in other scientific discussion. Psychoanalysis approaches the question of reality not as a given, predestined, objectifiable fact, nor as an existentialist concept. Although subjective reality for a subject of the unconscious is a bodily event, it is not simply the product of a subject's perception of an external stimulus. What, then, is the nature of reality for a subject of the unconscious, whose being cannot be excluded from his organic body?

DOI: 10.4324/9781003184799-1

For each subject, before his/her acquisition of language, the first Other is his or her own body. The body is the first reality encountered by each subject – the body which generates pain or dictates certain needs, which has an organic programme to survive and grow as well as being an essential medium to interact with the first significant others. On the other hand, when we are born with an organic body to a discourse, a position in the language is (or is not) available for us to claim. The subject of the unconscious faces this position through a fabricated reality: the unconscious fantasy. The fabric of the reality of language to which a subject is born is the mother tongue with its ambiguous and opaque nature. This reality is nothing but a raw and "morbid" material (the fabric of the Real), which will be used to fabricate a subjective knot of being.

The subject of the unconscious takes the first step towards fabricating a subjective reality when he claims a position – *carves* a position – in the ambiguous, primary jouissance. The morbid silence is broken by an act of guesswork originating from the unconscious. Finding a footing in the domain of language means that the subject has come to life, and what brings the subject to life is not physical birth, but this claiming of a space in language. To communicate his essential need and demand for love, a subject has to employ layers and properties of language besides learning the skills of speaking. He has to learn the new rules of the language. This is the moment in which he creates a myth (a subjective interpretation) of his being in the Other of language, a myth that he may continue to recite for many years to come. On the other hand, a subject might never want to engage with language, as happens in the case of the autist. In some radical cases of autism, the morbid fabric of the Real (the mother tongue) never elevates to an accessible form of fabricated reality and the biological body remains as a dead cage. So reality in psychoanalysis is always considered as a fabricated, subjective medium, through which the subject of the unconscious relates to the hole in the Other. The subject has agency to make a choice in relation to the Other, to engage in the game of guesswork with the Other and position himself in the available place in language, even if he chooses to refuse it all, which is to say that each subject finds a different way to face the Real.

I spent almost a decade studying the biological body in my medical training. For several years, I studied closely the physiological changes, the aetiology and pathology of diseases of the organs of the human body in the course of a lifetime. The questions of cause and origin of illness or a disturbance to the bodily homeostasis, how to prevent, avoid or postpone a medical condition, aging, senescence and death point to a single, libidinally invested motto: immortality. The immense interest and investment in today's market in promoting the motto of immortality – in fighting against mortality – is plain to see. It is an aspiration that goes far beyond living a healthier life for longer. The possibility of an immortal body suggests a simplistic interpretation of the human body, limiting it to the imaginary dimension. But in our era of "hyperreality" and the supremacy of symbolism and branding, such an approach to the question of subjectivity and the body should not come as a surprise. The approach of the neoliberal market to reality, subjectivity and promotion of a hope for immortality is at odds with the psychoanalytical approach. In psychoanalysis, for a subject of the unconscious, facing reality with a body and independent agency means facing one's own "mortality".

Besides the interest of the healthcare and cosmetics industries (the medical domain) in the biological body, there has been a rise of interest in the question of immortality in other fields – in robotics and information technology, as well as the worlds of art and entertainment, literature and media. Advances in medical technologies and artificial intelligence (AI) have even made it possible to take some steps in what might seem to be the direction of immortality. By contrast, in psychoanalysis, subjective reality makes the reality of a subject's "mortality" approachable. Nothing is more real than our mortality and our agency speaks precisely when we face the question of our mortality and find a way around it. Unlike any other clinical approaches, psychoanalysis helps the subject to face his mortality whenever possible and aims at promoting each subject's own way of fabricating a narrative around his mortal being. Psychoanalysis promotes a quite different motto from that of immortality. Psychoanalysis takes mortality and says: "This is something you cannot hide from".

The fabricated reality of the subject is the way he faces the bitter fact of his mortality. How to approach and navigate life depends on the subject's position towards his symptom, which is a self-made tool for coping with the opaque fabric of the Real into which we are born. My father had an important role in the first steps I took towards questioning the nature of my reality. His symbolic position in my mother's desire helped me to construct my symptom as a proxy against the Real of my mortality. I remember him saying: "Life is nothing but a bitter reality for everyone. What makes each of us different is how artfully we sweeten life's bitterness".

On the theme of the subject's creation of "reality", it is worth asking whether we can really draw a clear line between the subject's reality and that of the Other. If we agree on having an agency to create our version of reality, does the Other exist without a subject? The Lacanian Real is an opaque realm, from which a subject wants to escape by means of a symptom supported by a scenario in the unconscious – the fantasy. This Real can only be approached via a "fantasy" which is the closest analogy, from an analytical perspective, to the "reality". Is this not another way to say that we are born dead first? A subject can only come to life when he recognises his Other (first significant Other/care giver) and realises a lack in this Other. He then relates to the lack/hole in the Other by fabricating a fantasy, which is unconscious (it is not the same as imagination). The fantasy saves the subject from the anguish of a radical encounter with the questions of his sexuality and mortality.

Struck by my father's response to my question, I remember that I started concocting and telling stories to others about myself, my birth and my parents' relationship and began to picture myself in an imaginary future. Many of those stories were revised and altered during my analysis. The space created by psychoanalysis encouraged me to question the nature of my reality as a subject, my ability to refashion my symptom through my own agency. Psychoanalysis offers a space to elaborate our ethics and our position in relation to the Other, what we want to be and what we can become as an intelligent speaking being that owes its existence to an interaction with two Others – body and language. Questioning the nature of our reality might make us decide to deconstruct the entire world that we have built around us. Where a subject positions himself in relation to perceiving, interpreting and manipulating external reality is precisely what psychoanalysis targets and what it is interested in. When a subject claims his position and constructs his reality, it is through constructing a purpose of his being (the symptom), with which he then moves through life. If this life purpose fails to maintain a meaningful existence for the subject in his sexualised and civilised body, he might choose to question all the fabricated myths that he had once created for life's journey. In such a case, psychoanalysis provides space for a deep analysis of the subjective position: for revisiting, deconstructing, remodelling and, finally, shaping a new reality.

I decided to write this text soon after I lost my father. Why did his loss bring me anguish and fright rather than, for example, a deep regret, guilt or sadness? As if all my attempts to sweeten the bitterness of life had collapsed. Some life events can, indeed, shake up a subject's reality and leave him no concealment from the anguish-provoking Real. My father's passing brought me face to face once again with the question of my own mortality. By the time I finished writing this text, I stood in a better place in my grief. Through revisiting and analysing the status of my symptom, my position in language was once again questioned, decomposed and gradually reconstructed.

When I heard of his death, which was unexpected and came as a shock, I felt no emotion. The reaction came from by body. Under the hot sun of southern France, my whole body shook uncontrollably. I remember little of what happened around me during the first few hours after hearing the news. It seemed impossible that he should have gone so soon. I was angry and in denial. I and my family, dressed in black, remembered him with a glass of his favourite red French wine, while listening to his favourite music. I immersed myself in the various tasks that had to be done in connection with his death, while at the same time trying to come to terms with my loss. After a month, back home in London, I fell ill with an illness similar to his. As if my body had begun to grieve, the body which "enjoys itself" independently: "Cela se jouit", as Lacan tells us. My feelings ranged from blankness, lack of focus, to anger and sadness, at the same time as my body fought the nuisance of illness. I experienced the rush of work and pace of life in London as a welcome distraction. The process of mourning is said to have stages and I knew that my task was to acknowledge to myself the reality of the loss. My family, friends and colleagues offered a shoulder to cry on – the work of mourning cannot be solitary. In my dreams, he would be there one night, fully alive, but another night dead. My thoughts raced to explore my past in order to find out what had gone with him. I tried to remind myself that my pain was not privileged or more precious than anybody else's pain, and that I was not the only person who mourned, but to no avail.

I reflected on my father's journey in life and found mine deeply intertwined with his. My father was all about moving – leaving and returning. All my life, I remember him going away, but then – each time – coming back. Being arrested and detained soon after the 1979 revolution (an experience from which he never fully recovered), or his numerous health issues since his youth, he remained young in spirit and a great sufferer all his life. He was unable to complete his medical degree, and I completed this unfinished task by graduating from medical school. He wanted to become a surgeon, or a psychiatrist offering a "talking cure". I changed my path from surgery to become an analyst. He wanted to come to the UK to study and now I am a Londoner. He took a passionate interest in the Cannes Film Festival and I do not miss a summer to catch up with my writing near Cannes. He was my first teacher in creative writing, and I eventually wrote a book in my father-tongue (sent for publication on the morning of his funeral). His dream had provided foundations for my way of living and his gaze was now shut down. I challenged destiny over the years in analysis to form my own desirable mode of being, but only on those foundations. This time he was gone with no possibility of return, and it was as if I had gone with him.

My father and I had mirrored each other for many years. His presence and his gaze had found meaning in my preoccupation with the phoenix myth – a departure, always followed by a return – as a fantasy support of my symptom. In the news of his death, it was as if I had departed with him. This became clear to me when, after a long wait during which I felt either nothing or mere sadness, a blaze of anguish took me by surprise and overcame me. From drinking wine in his memory in Monte Carlo to a long walk that it took in Windsor, I knew that I had to be patient with the pain of loss. But the agony of anguish took no interest in that. Certain knowledge is easily defeated by anguish. I had experienced this affect before, in another episode of symbolic separation from him, and my personal journey in psychoanalysis had begun soon after it. A particular image that had occurred to me then was repeated now in my new experience of anguish: the gates of our family garden of pomegranates opened and my father at the end of the garden stood pouring himself a drink. He went inside with his glass and a drought garden haunted all my senses. The desert of reality cornered me and the question of mortality arose once more. Now, he is back in my new reality. The marker of the Real (the anguish) has long gone. In this new reality, his presence is remembered and will live on through words.

Soon after my father's death came the COVID-19 pandemic. It was felt as a moment of interruption. Interruption of the continuation of enjoyment. The pandemic brought a variety of responses in each of us, all based on a subjective reality supported by an unconscious fantasy. Our everyday reality suddenly changed. The feelings we heard of in the psychoanalytic clinic ranged from fear to guilt to anguish. The fear of deprivation, of not having enough food and other essentials (toilet paper!), which corresponds to the Freudian oral drive; the fear of being restricted, limited or infantilised (the anal drive); the guilt of contaminating loved ones and others (which may point to an underlying desire to contaminate them), entailing avoidance and phobia of public places and people or the anguish of not knowing what lay ahead for the subject. One analysand spoke to me of the unbearable shame she felt in her work place at being diagnosed with COVID-19. Many looked for an agent (the Other) who could be held accountable for the situation. Laying blame on certain groups of people was used as a way of tackling the guilt, and this even went as far as racist attacks, such as that on a Singaporean student in the west end of London in February 2020. The anxiety of not knowing what the future held or when the pandemic would go away was very present in the clinic, particularly in the first few weeks of the lockdown, and also as public places began to reopen a few months later.

What we heard from the psychoanalytical couch was the way in which each subject dealt with his unsettling feelings and the uncanny in the body. It may seem, to outward appearances, that we reacted or behaved similarly in the face of adversity, but the effect of the pandemic was received in a particular way by each of us depending on how each subject had woven his mode of being in the language and how his body seeks pleasure. A single event can be read in various ways by a subject with a mortal and sexualised body. Where a subject positions himself in the language, how he forms his ethical stance towards the Other and how he gains his agency during the crisis once again reminded us of the futility of trying to predict and generalise a course of action in a human society. We might have reacted similarly at the level of behaviour patterns, but certainly for different reasons. A subjective position towards the symbolic lack in the Other means that an unconscious strategy is at work in coping with this lack: to accept or reject (negate) it. There are different ways to negotiate terms and find a compromise with the desiring Other.

Some refused to follow the government's instructions or protested against all or some of the rules. In Freud's work, it is precisely refusal and contestation that signify a subjective agency. In the clinic of psychoanalysis, it is not uncommon to hear an echo of contestation from time to time on the side of the analysand when, for example, he or she is late or misses a session or a payment. One of my patients told me that, during her potty training, she had once fallen asleep in the toilet for more than an hour, while the rest of the family, unaware where she was, searched for her in a state of growing panic. She often complained of falling physically ill when approaching deadlines at work that she was expected to meet. She had a strict mother with rigid rules about times for eating and sleeping. Later in life, whenever she was situated in some major interaction with the Other, her body responded with an illness, or she stayed in bed and slept. As if the only space where she could exercise agency over her own timing was in her sleep, as when she had fallen asleep on the toilet in childhood.

So, the subjectivity we understand from a psychoanalytical perspective is not the product of a direct effect coming from the culture or from a discourse. The national strategies and responses of countries and governments to the pandemic have differed according to differences in culture. The question of mortality arose again but was mainly reduced to statistics – the number of deaths in each country by the governments. The 2020 pandemic will certainly leave an invisible mark on contemporary culture, a mark that may even lead to the formation of a different social bond between speaking beings in the future. With what effect and, more importantly, in what way would the new social bond be interpreted by the subject of the unconscious? How would the subjective interpretation appear in the symptom of the next generation? These are questions which psychoanalysis is interested in and can approach. Perhaps we need more time to wait and learn from the bodily events that arise at the start of the new decade from the experience of the pandemic. A common, transcultural motto, heard from different generations in face of the crisis was "how to survive". Some suffered from physical and mental pain, others experienced overpowering anxiety over the loss of loved ones, and others simply enjoyed the enforced leisure.

Our attitude towards the question of our death might be described as perverse. We know that we will die one day, but we disavow the fact. So we have a double knowledge: we die but we do not die. This knowledge can haunt us in our adult life, when we are trapped in a situation where we experience the marks of primary jouissance – an experience where a subject is cornered and cannot move or recognise his agency. 2020 might also be called the year of "Nobody knows" or perhaps the year of "No, body knows". For some, the body attested to a knowledge, which could no longer be disavowed: that of mortality. It is the year when the Lacanian concept of sexual non-rapport – non-rapport between two Real bodies – found tangible meaning.

The pandemic reality can also be interpreted as a moment in history where the reality of some subjects suddenly became everyone's reality. For example, walking through an eerily empty central London reminded me of a sci-fi movie by Christopher Nolan, *Inception*. In the dream of protagonists, all the buildings of their city were abandoned or deserted. It also reminded me of my mother's account of the aftermath of the 1979 revolution in Iran, when all the public places of celebration and entertainment, dance and music, cinema and theatres, wineries and bars, clubs and brothels were closed down overnight. Fundamentalism became a virus eating through the flesh of culture or any symbol of freedom for men and women (particularly for women). Womanhood was reduced to an object of sin and temptation. Kisses and hugs in public spaces were forbidden. The same echo could be heard in an evening in late March 2020. I felt once again for my parents' generation.

The COVID-19 pandemic crystallised another question for me: that of space and the Real body. 2020 was a year when a subject's life and death were overshadowed by numbers and statistics. It can also be called the year of the screen (but not the big magical screen of cinema, which was sorely missed!), because, as well as targeting the body directly, the virus also cut the body off from its real presence in the social bond, reducing it to an image in video calls.

Indeed the body knew that our subjective reality was changing. Not simply because it became unfit, fatter or thinner, not simply due to lack of movement and various scientific and medical facts. The Real body was not fooled by the screen and software applications. The sexual non-rapport and mortality of the subject are approached via subjective reality in terms of how to deal with such a non-rapport and with the anguish that arises from it. When the question of mortality was approached without the mediation of a proxy (a fantasy), the body knew what was happening. The Real body of the speaking being experienced an overwhelming anxiety or responded through bodily symptoms. Although some of us tried to maintain our social life by means of internet and social media, this could only support a minimal aspect of the subject's social bond with the Other. The sexual non-rapport can only be mediated by the agency of the subject, and it takes time for each subject to produce a subjective knowledge for the gap in the Real, a knowledge that can help the subject to find his new grip in the new reality/normality.

How did the pandemic affect the clinic of psychoanalysis when many analysts continue working remotely during this period?

In 2020 psychoanalysts had more experience than ever before of working remotely. The pandemic created space for a forced encounter with the controversial question of long date whether online/telephone sessions are possible/effective/ethical. Working remotely during the pandemic was a new and tiring reality for many of us. Some of us liked to think that the current role of the telephone and electronic media as place holders for analytical sessions would not last. But what would happen to psychoanalysis if the work stayed remote?

What interests me is not the practicality of remote analysis because that seems to me the wrong focus. It is dangerous and misleading to think only about the practicality and possibility of remote analysis, because then we are thinking only about matters of everyday reality and – as we are well aware, from a psychoanalytical perspective the very essence of reality can be inverted, distorted and the opposite of everyday reality.

I won't focus here either on the analyst's symptom, which allows each analyst to occupy and sustain his or her position. For example, some analysts can be better listeners to the unconscious over the phone or online, because they find it easier in those circumstances to focus on the words of the analysand. There are analysts whose core of symptom echoes an enjoyment around the act of 'moving' and who seem quite happy to conduct analysis remotely for this reason. Psychoanalysts have found more ways and more creative ways to pursue their trade from virtual offices/spaces during the recent pandemic, and this shift may even be permanent for some of them. For some psychoanalysts the pandemic has brought a wished-for resolution of doubts about going online, moving abroad or giving up their offices.

Our focus here, however, will be on examining different elements of the analytic discourse, and for this purpose it would perhaps be useful to be reminded once again of what is really at stake in an analytical relationship between analyst and analysand. Let us start with the fundamental question: can analysis conducted remotely work for the speaking being, where the Real unconscious and Real body are engaged remotely? The same sort of question can be raised for remote training. How can analytic training, which differs from other types of training in the field, approach the question of formation in psychoanalysis when it is carried out remotely? As discussed in Lacan's 17th seminar (Lacan, 1969–70), the formation of the analyst involves a realisation of the impossibility of coincidence between truth and any kind of knowledge. When Lacan puts the object a in the position of the agent in the analytic discourse and the divided subject in the field of the Other, he reminds us that the product of analytic work is not a form of knowledge, unless it is a particular kind of "hidden knowledge" – the truth of our being which is obtained when, through the analyst's interpretation of the analysand's narrative, the unary trait (S1) is spoken. This produced knowledge would then allow the subject of the unconscious to approach sexual non-rapport. We will discuss this in more depth in the chapter on diagnosis.

My intention here is to emphasise that we should not forget the aim of analysis, regardless of the context in which we work on the unconscious. We start from the position of the analyst, a position that enables the emergence of the moment of enunciation for each subject of the unconscious – a moment where a subject is manifested. The position of the analyst (at the level of the transference, as an "agalma holder", but not only there) is the space where the analytical act – the cut, the surprise, the arrest – originates. In every analytic setting, it is the *transference* which facilitates the Real effect of analytical acts targeting the analysand's unconscious. The analytical act (cut and punctuations) can only be effective if it comes from a position which is both recognised and sanctioned in the analysand's transference. In other words, there has to be trust in this position as an agalma holder, enabling the cut which targets the subject's everyday narrative in order for him to move towards certain unconscious truth/knowledge about subjectivity. This truth, which, according to Lacan, is always half said (mi-dire), concerns the following: our mode of relating to the Other's desire as a social being; our way/purpose in life (symptom) separating us from a primary jouissance (the fabric of the Real) on which we have founded our unique way of being; our way of dealing with urges of morbid jouissance (the reminder of our mortality); finding a way to relate to the sexual non-rapport in our relationships with significant others; and how to find a compromise with our sexuality, if sexual ambiguity is problematic. The question, then, is whether working remotely affects the dynamic of the transference.

There are cases when remote work gives definite transference advantages. In my work with a case of perversion, online communication helped and boosted a useful transference by giving sufficient distance from the analyst. The symbolic distance made the perverse subject less anxious. He said: "I can have a conversation with you without experiencing constant urges to cross a boundary". He was trying to find another way to regain his agency over his life other than putting himself in a masochistic position. Punctuating the work (i.e. ending sessions) remotely was challenging at the beginning, but being in his own space had apparently reduced the anguish of a physical encounter with women. Such encounters were a new dilemma for him in his social life after a fallout with a female colleague at work. He said that she constantly imposed more tasks on him, making it impossible to cope with the work load. He then suddenly developed a physical condition that resulted in a long illness and hospitalisation. More details from his personal and professional life made him more conscious of his tendency to indulge in a morbid mode of jouissance which put him in positions that required much work and effort for very little return. He interpreted those tasks as doing a favour for others. By contrast, the analytic arrangement, where he received a session in return for payment, helped to organise access to an accessible form of enjoyment. By intimidating those around him and cutting them off from his daily life, he had engineered a situation where he appeared to the victim of the whole world by perceiving the reaction of others to such treatment as his punishment. After recovering from his physical illness, he had given up agency over his own everyday life to others. All his daily chores and arrangements were set and organised by the Other. "I am a puppet of my partner", he said. These new arrangements in his household had pushed him further into the destructive mode of jouissance induced by his masochistic position.

How exactly did remote work help the direction of the treatment in this case by enabling the subject to approach the hole in the Other differently than by a perverse act? He was reminded of his agency over the choices he had in every social bond, including online sessions, when I asked him to send me the Zoom invitation on a few occasions. Remote sessions gave him a space to reflect on his past, temporarily freeing him from uncontrollable urges, which were his main torturing preoccupation. Once in a session he said that he was not upset when he was cut short by other people when speaking, clearly treating such incidents as a "soft" punishment. When that session came to an end, I waited for him to press the "leave the meeting" button.

The solution for a pervert is the problem. As a consequence of disavowing the deprivation in the Other, a perverse subject forms an act (a perverse act) to defend himself against the overwhelming, primary jouissance in his union with the Other. The online space gave this subject a much-needed break to consider another strategy for coming to terms with the hole in the Other. He found a way to question his stance towards a destructive mode of jouissance. It is interesting to speculate how that could be achieved in sessions held in person. Would it be possible, in face-to-face encounters, to create a dynamic such that the subject could see through the perverse act and modify, cope with or change it? This question gave me pause.

When the lockdown happened, analysts were advised not to see people in person where possible in obedience to the national regulations. For a long-term obsessional analysand, emphasis on travelling to my office had been a way to let his symptom speak to him. So it seemed as if the lockdown situation would not facilitate the analytical act and would be a challenge to the continuity of the work. Surprisingly, the fact that he no longer had to travel to sessions made this particular subject question the status of his symptom as linked to the chore of travelling to my practice. As if he had realised for the first time (after experiencing a moment of interruption to the usual way of things) why there had been an emphasis on travelling. He started to have more frequent sessions despite his previous resistance to doing so. The previous regularity had become part of a subject's routine,

discours de l'analysté

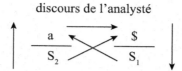

Figure 0.2a Discours de l'analyste

discours de l'analysté

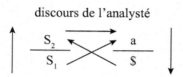

Figure 0.2b Discours de l'université

and reducing the Other's desire to a routine demand was his way of coping with the hole in the Other. When the presence of the analyst becomes part of a subject's routine rather than being taken as a challenging position towards the happenings of everyday life, the position of the analyst and his acts, which need to be directed towards the subject's division, instead become a fix or repair. The analytic discourse then makes a clockwise move to the academic discourse where knowledge is the agent rather than being a product that allows the subject to approach his mortality while becoming more able to access jouissance (Lacan, 1969–70, pp. 99 and 104).

Another analysand was angry when she learned that I would be working remotely during the lockdown. She was somebody who did not play by the rules that her own body dictated. She was almost constantly ill or under the weather due to extreme experiments with her physical appearance and health. Interventions such as various approaches to boosting her physical energy, dieting, surgery, invasive and non-invasive cosmetic interventions were her way of accessing her body. She had an unusual relation to physical pain. As if she had to get rid of the pain as quickly as possible, since it caused her to panic. So that her phobia of pain itself generated a painful experience. In her approach to her body, she seemed to want to challenge the laws of nature, against which she had to protect herself.

After her outburst of anger at the lockdown rules on a WhatsApp call, I asked her what would be changed for her? She replied: "My body won't be on your couch. Isn't it the first rule of analysis?" I cut the session by saying: "You don't play by the rules".

I had tried several times before then to pinpoint her symptomatic approach to the meaning of her body, health and mortality, but my words had not carried weight. This time, however, a radical cut of the Imaginary body (not being on the couch), an absence of physical space made her hear for the first time an echo of her symptom in relation to pain and the body. It was not necessarily the analyst's voice on a WhatsApp call that achieved this. Rather the subject of the unconscious was stirred by being removed from the usual setting and arrangement of the analysis. As if the position of the analyst had targeted the Real body in its absence, an absence which had worked productively for the analysand's unconscious.

The question then is: did we address the Real body while working remotely? Did the analytic act cut through everyday nonsense? I would like to think that it did.

In this book, you may find some thoughts on the Lacanian subject: what are we as a speaking being? What makes us a human subject from a psychoanalytic perspective? Is it feelings and affect that make us a human? Or was it the Freudian invention of the unconscious that drew a line between human and a non-human?

What can be learnt from the subject of the unconscious in the clinic of psychoanalysis that can help us to approach these questions? In the chapters that follow, I have taken examples from the clinic of psychoanalysis as well as cultural references (ranging from ancient Persia to Theatreland of London 2020) from the art of cinema, poetry and handcrafts, in order to elaborate once again the question of subjectivity, reality and truth from a psychoanalytical perspective. In the era of hyperreality, the agency of branding and marketing strategies has overshadowed the reality of a human being, his true nature and agency. The hyperreality of contemporary society creates in each individual a false hope of becoming a high-fidelity copy of their idols, and such a fallacy has led many to believe that this is what determines their being in a social bond. In the book I explore the question of the reality and mortality of a subject through a Lacanian prism, from the theorising of analytical subjectivity that starts with the Freudian Oedipal myth more than a century ago to the futurist aspiration to fabricate human beings according to some ideal model.

Lacan's trajectory regarding the theory of the unconscious has been much commented on. Lacan elaborated on how understandings and misunderstandings of what was referred to (following Freud) as the "unconscious" impacted on the politics and practical clinic of psychoanalysis. The "unconscious" is also a prime example of a Freudian term that is in use today outside psychoanalysis with a quite different meaning from that which Freud intended. It is one of the most familiar terms heard in and from the public domain (although the "sub-conscious" is currently the more popular term). It is used in medicine to describe a state of not being awake or aware of one's senses; scientists working on artificial intelligence also use the term for a concept that, it is hoped, will be applicable for improving the human-like abilities of robotic AI.

It is interesting to note that Freud's first topic – the "iceberg" model – has found extensive attention and popularity, while the second topic, from which Lacan's reinvention starts, has become a model for many modern talking therapies, used to orient the direction of treatment. Lacan's efforts to revisit and reinvent the concept of the unconscious do not merely reflect his interest in linguistics and the philosophy of structuralism. The Lacan of the 1960s already had long experience of the clinic, which had taught him – and, therefore, us today – that blaming repression and so-called human instinctive conflicts is over-simplistic and will result in failures in the analyst's efforts to analyse the material, as he attempts to avoid stagnation and repetition of the work. We, humans, have the benefits of understanding and knowledge, which give us power and motivation and which pacify us in our mode of life. Speaking – as one aspect of language – is both our privilege and our doom. Simple models and making life simple are a much-loved trend today. However, there are moments – moments that Freud, in the late nineteenth century, already noticed – which remind us of our cognitive blindness and inability to explain certain human conditions. This was felt (by Freud) in the clinic of a suffering subject. The concept of the unconscious has been invented and discussed before Freud, in philosophy, but with other connotations. And, several decades after Freud's second topic, researchers in the field of the psyche tried inventing all sort of new explanations in order to name what was experienced in the clinic of the "speaking being". The focus of the next chapter will be the concept of the unconscious in psychoanalysis.

In the third chapter, we approach the question of "the symptom". "Symptom" is a term that has been overshadowed by the politics of health and care systems. It is equated with a condition of disease or an underlying issue which calls for a health professional's intervention. For Freud and psychoanalysis, however, a symptom is a condition that cannot be taken away from the apparatus of human subjectivity. We cannot continue to live our reality without a symptom. The formation of the symptom shows our subjective agency, which can lead or not lead to separation of the subject from the Other. Later, the status of the symptom can be challenged and changed through a subject's life journey. The symptom is what offers a subject a purpose in life and translates a mode of jouissance for him. If the act of translation fails, the subject is faced with his mortality, which is experienced as pain at the level of body. Symptom formation is marked by the discourse in which we live, because the fabric from which a symptom originates (the fabric of the Real or mother tongue in the Lacanian sense) is marked by culture. For example, the generation born into digital technology and social media (the demographic cohort of the "Z" generation born since the mid- to late-1990s), may well shape a symptom that is quite different from that of previous and earlier generations, in order to give coherence to their subjectivity in the light of the internet and virtual space. But a different status for the symptom does not mean a radical shift in the concept of subjectivity in psychoanalysis. Rather it is a question of finding a different medium in order to keep our ethical stance in the language.

A few years ago, I moved my London office to a new location. My new office had apparently been a butcher's shop for a long period from the early twentieth century until the mid-1970s. I did not know the history of the place until one of my patients told me something about the history of the neighbourhood. A gothic theme-story behind a consulting room, I thought to myself! Then, I realised that what happens to an analysand's symptom during and after an analysis is no less than a butchering of the status of the symptom. An analysand's symptom is "butchered", it is "hacked about" in order to make something different: what Lacan calls the "sinthomee". As a new translator of the jouissance particular to each subject, the sinthome makes the reality of a subject meaningful and purposeful.

In the chapter on fairy tales and subjectivity, I have explored the effect of fairy tales on the formation of the subject. The narratives of fairy tales, for example, are one possible metaphorical way to recount to ourselves the problematic issues, challenges, beauties or complications found in our social being. They have a "gothic" language, in the sense of dealing with horror and anguish. They are born out of the creative, innovative human mind – the work of lovers of fantasy and metaphor. A fairy in a fairy tale functions as a space to project dreams, thoughts and immense frustration. Humans, as speaking beings, manage to constantly invent new forms of narration. We speak differently about our dreams and phantasies in analysis. We address ourselves through media beyond words and meanings. We become able to understand the language in which the unconscious is represented (lalangue). We sing the verses of an unwritten poetry that is knotted into the very core of our being. A poetry that is untranslatable in any language, since it is a woven narrative – a character that ultimately makes it so precious to each one of us. Psychoanalysis is the art of enabling a subject to listen to a silence. Then this silence is transformed into the notes of a written melody, an unnamed refrain, which will be heard and sung by the subject of the unconscious until it falls silent again. Once the castle of psychoanalysis has been explored chamber by chamber, one might not want to leave it behind. Perhaps we might look for role models elsewhere. Or, perhaps, we might immerse ourselves completely in the world of fantasy, dive into a tale so deeply that, eventually, we feel safe.

Could you locate Cinderella, Rapunzel, Sleeping Beauty and Belle of *Beauty and the Beast* somewhere in the above paragraph?

We will continue with a chapter on the question of diagnosis. I have attempted to elaborate the question of clinical diagnosis and to show how an understanding of different psychical structures is important in clinical psychoanalysis. This is not a matter of compartmentalising the lives of subjects based on certain pre-ordained categories. Rather, it is a matter of how we, as psychoanalysts, position ourselves in relation to the narrative that we receive in each particular case.

What is central to the question of subjectivity in psychoanalysis is the body. The Real body has been much elaborated and discussed in the literature of psychoanalysis. In the sixth chapter we will try to raise some questions regarding the concept of the Other jouissance in Lacan's work and the Real body. How and for what reason does a subject experience excitation at the level of his body? What does such an experience tell a subject about his sexual position in the language? Both Freud and Lacan believed that what is needed here is the concept of the drive, which connects the body to the unconscious – the unconscious, which was invented by Freud to examine certain truths about human subjectivity.

In the final chapter, I look at how the concept of psychoanalytic affects in ancient Persian literature relate to more contemporary narratives on the question of sexuality. It is an established truism that feelings and emotions are what make us humane. But how should psychoanalysis respond to such phenomenon when, for example, human feelings and excitations can be learned by AI or by a high-fidelity replica of whatever is referred to as a human being? Lacan gives anxiety a privileged position amongst the affects, linking it with the reality of subjectivity: that is, mortality. The anguish I experienced during my recent grief over my father's death, followed by the shock of the COVID-19 pandemic, made me face the question of my own mortality as well as my ethical stance as a subject and speaking being in the language, thereby leading to the birth of this text.

London, Fitzrovia, July 2020

To the memories of my father and his kindness to animals and the nature

Bibliography

Lacan, J. (1969–70). *The seminar of Jacque Lacan: Book XVII: The other side of Psychoa-nalysis*. Russell Grigg (Trans.). London: Norton.

Figure 1.1 The Unconscious, photograph by Bardia Moeini

Chapter 1

Freud's second topic and the Lacanian subject of the unconscious

Introduction

How did Freud's theorising approach the concept of the subject? Where did Lacan start to formulate his concept of the unconscious? Where is the unconscious situated in a topological formation, and what happened to the Lacanian theory of the unconscious (towards the end of Lacan's teaching)? I will approach these questions by examining the different potentialities in Freud's second topic (Freud, 1923) through Lacan's critique of the Freudian unconscious, which led him to conceptualise his transgressive subject of the unconscious and, later, the concept of the speaking being or "parlêtre".

The high castle of psychoanalysis was built on the hill of the unconscious. Freud's invention of the unconscious opened up a space to explore what we are as speaking beings. The concept of the unconscious as discovered or invented by Freud was not a philosophical construct, nor did it accept medical views on consciousness and unconsciousness. The Freudian unconscious and its formations (dream, bungled action, lapsus and symptom) were worked through by Lacan in a way that led him to theorise the subject of the unconscious as something very different from the Cartesian subject, as a subject whose unconscious defies any philosophical understanding. The Lacanian subject is a sexed being who has agency over the formation of the symptom and montage of the drive, a subject who comes into being with a mortal body. The subject's drives – with their repetitive and excessive nature – originate from certain zones/area in the body and are marked by the culture which he is born into.

Now, if the enjoyment gained through the drive montage in the endeavour to trick the Real of sexuality fails the subject, leaving him in pain and anguish, he might find himself before the gate of the castle of psychoanalysis. The gate is the "transference", which brings him inside the castle. The password that is needed in order to gain admission to the castle – the moment when he becomes an analysand – is the manner in which he subjectifies his suffering. It is only after an exhaustive tour of the castle, built upon the unconscious, that the Real of the sexual non-rapport (in Lacan's expression) can become more tolerable for the subject. At the end of analysis, the explored castle, which was previously known as the castle of

DOI: 10.4324/9781003184799-2

psychoanalysis, become something different – it is converted into the subject's own way of dealing with his sexuality and mortality, that is his "sinthome". The sinthome would be his new purpose in life, giving a meaningful position in the language to his being, to his three-dimensional being consisting of Real, Symbolic and Imaginary (Lacan, 1975–6).

The concept of the subject from Freud to Lacan

If one had to locate Freud's second topic inside the castle of psychoanalysis, it would surely be found in the cellar – a room where one finds dysfunctional, abandoned objects and sees some potential use in them. Freud's semi-topological representation of the psyche is just such an archaic object with potential. Although the second topic is a structurally fundamental model, it is not as functional as it could be. It required, not complete demolition, but more or less substantial reworking. Lacan's first and second seminars would not have been possible if there had not been great potential in Freud's second topic, and Lacan's later theories on R, S and I (developed through the 1950s and 1960s) crystallised around his critique of the Freudian model of ego, id and superego.

The second topic could not entirely resolve Freud's interest and puzzlement over the existential dilemma of a civilised man (mortality) and of his relation to an accessible form of enjoyment (jouissance). But the topic was capable of a reworking and reformulation that took it further in that direction, as Lacan showed when he approached the question of the formation of the subject. It is from the second topic that Lacan begins his work on the subject of the unconscious.

Lacan offers an alternative reading of the second topic, not as a structural model of the psyche consisting of three agencies – a strict ego, forbidding superego and an unruly id, with a more or less competent ego doing its best to mediate between them, but as a foundational model of the subject of the unconscious, theorised by Lacan in terms of his three orders of the Imaginary, Symbolic and Real.

The Freudian "ego" was considered by Lacan to be partially unconscious and was certainly not equated by him with the subject (Lacan, 1953–4). In Lacan's work, a subject appears in language through an "enunciation" at a precise moment of surprise. Is this where Freud's idea of "id" comes into play? Or, is it only due to the ego's incompetence in performing its principal act of censorship that such "being" manifests itself? Where is the unconscious to be found in the second model of the psyche? To approach these questions, Lacan in the early 1950s introduces his "L schema" as his first topological representation of the subject (Lacan, 1954–5). The L schema consists of four elements (ego, other, subject and Other) and emphasises the Symbolic dimension over the Imaginary. This is the first topological model in Lacan's work to theorise the formation of the subject in language. The Other of the subject is language, and it is where subjectivity is constituted. Here, the Freudian id coincides with Lacan's subject as "I", but not as "me" or ego. The relation between the ego and the Other is in the Imaginary dimension, while the subject and the Other are linked in the Symbolic register.

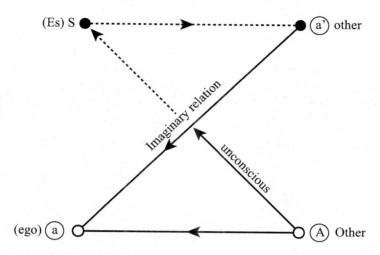

Figure 1.2 L schema

When developing his theory of the subject in the early 1950s, Lacan started with the two agencies of "ego" and "id" from Freud's second model. He came to an exploration and reformulation of the super-ego in the 7th seminar, later in the same decade. The Freudian triadic structure – a non-topological formation – that had been left in the cellar of psychoanalysis became a foundation for Lacan's theory of the formation of the subject, via the mirror phase and identification, the use of topological objects such as the interior 8, the Möbius strip representation of the unconscious, the torus to show the structure of the subject and the concept of extimacy, developments around the theme of ethics, and the famous command to "Enjoy!", leading finally to Lacan's elaborated work on R, S and I, the object *a*, the sinthome, the Real unconscious and parlêtre.

If Freud's *Interpretation of Dreams* is considered the bible of Freudianism, Lacan's 11th Seminar in 1964 can be viewed as foundational for all of Lacan's work from that time onwards. It is where Lacan reinvents psychoanalysis, although there is much in previous seminars that demonstrate his desire to challenge what he saw as misunderstandings of Freud's legacy and to establish a firm platform for what was referred to as "psychoanalysis". He had elaborated the concept of the unconscious using the media of linguistics and topology on several occasions prior to 1964. He had emphasised the impossibility of articulation, of naming absolutely everything. What makes the 11th Seminar particularly significant is that it marks Lacan's break with and turning away from the Freudian unconscious as outlined in the second topic. If the Lacanian "subject" had already been con-ceptualised to some extent, the term is now used for the first time in place of the "unconscious". Lacan's famous phrase: "the unconscious is structured like a language" (used and misinterpreted over and over again, to this day) pales alongside the significance of his reinvention, which gave birth to a new idea of the subject – a subject, which, as an effect of language, goes through alienation and separation and then forms a desire in relation to a lack in the Other and enjoys the montage of the drive. According to Lacan, the subject begins to appear by realising his existence as separate from the Other. Such a realisation and separation always have a price for the subject. The residue of primary jouissance will remain. We will return to this later.

The unconscious, then, which is and remains an essentially Freudian term, is located by Lacan in the field of the Other. Lacan, unlike some other post-Freudian interpreters of the concept of the unconscious, did not believe that the unconscious is merely the result of repression and that it has a "primordial", "archaic" and "instinctual" nature. The repetition and resistance that occur in the course of an analysis testify to an active mode of agency in the field of the Other. The subject in analysis has an unconscious with a pulsation and inconsistency, his being is inscribed by a lack of being (manque-à-être) in relation to the Other. In other words, the subject in his very core is not independent of the Other. But, on the other hand, there is no Other without a subject.

In the early 1960s, Lacan defined the subject of the unconscious as what one signifier represents for another signifier. Lacan's teachings on the unconscious, at this stage, revolve around the manifestation of the subject in gaps or splits, the "béance" where the unconscious is. This idea coincides with the presence of the unconscious in the field of the Other having an inconsistent "pulsation". Precisely this was the justification for Lacan's practice of cutting sessions short – making them of variable length, which became a matter of dispute between him and the IPA. A cut at the precise moment of pulsation saves and guarantees the continuity of a course of analysis. It is a cut at a "béance" – not a termination of the present session but rather the start of the next.

The question here would be when or, to be more precise, *from where* the analyst should decide upon a cut. This concerns the question of where the cut is made. Lacan's idea in the 11th Seminar is that it is made at moments of uncertainty, when the unconscious is enunciated, at moments when the thinking ego fails and the subject of the unconscious speaks. Once in a session, as a response to an "enunciation" by the analysand, I stood up and terminated the session without saying a word, and did so automatically, without giving it a thought. Such an action by the analyst causes surprise on both sides – for the analyst and for the analysand – and produces a certain unconscious knowledge. It is, in fact, a formation of the unconscious as found in the analytical space between two speaking beings.

The aim of the analyst's act is not simply the return of the repressed. The return of the repressed signifies a mark of jouissance on the body. The analytical act targets the structure of the subject where it has come into being for potential transformation. The analyst is a subject who has already worked or is working on the subject of the unconscious in another space, yet again, with another subject of the unconscious. In his own consulting room, he is another subject whose unconscious is the Other for that of the analysand. They are working both in and on the unconscious that exists between them (Harari, 2004). As such, the unconscious is another name for what we call "the clinical work". The analyst does not induce or create it from the position of analyst, but, with the help of transference, he creates a space where the birth of the unconscious can happen. Similar to a midwife – he delivers the unconscious. Lacan used the Möbius strip as a representation of the subject of the unconscious. The surface of the Möbius strip is not divided between inner and outer sides, and it thus illustrates the return of the repressed as well as the analytical cut (interpretation) that aims at transforming rather than dissolving the subject of the unconscious – the cut, which goes against the repetitive continuation of the subject's narratives and complaints. Such transformation targets the core of the subject's primary division or loss: the unary trait. The unary trait, which had stood for the loss of the Thing, supports the subject, but the subject disappears when the unary trait appears. So the unary trait stands for a double loss.

According to Lacan, the subject, coming from a union, first passes through an alienation. The subject is called on to choose between bad and worse: "your money or your life!" Alienation and separation are two operations, which result in the formation of the subject of the unconscious. After alienation, which results in the subject's division, the subject has to go through a separation in order to form a desire in relation to the lack in the Other. In this operation, according to Lacan, S1 (as "the first signifier, the unary signifier" (Lacan, 1963–4, p. 218) produced in the mechanism of alienation) is replaced by the *objet a* as the cause of desire. While S1 stands for a loss, the object *a* stands for a lack in the Other, which ultimately causes the subject's desire. In alienation, the divided and "fading" subject is faced with S1 as the first representation of the subject for another signifier in the signifying chain, while in the operation of separation, the subject comes face to face with "the weak point" of the signifying articulation. This weak point, in Lacan's words, is in fact another name for the *objet a*. So the S1 is the signifier of the first loss in the operation of alienation and the *objet a* is the lost object of the Other's jouissance. In the course of analysis, the subject is helped to find some solution to this lack; a lack that results from separation and, in addition, is pushed towards alienation and primary loss. To choose or not to choose one's alienation/division in life is to go in a contrary direction along the earlier path that led to the birth of the subject; a subject that always remains barred.

As an attempt to clarify this, let us take a clinical example:

A few years ago, I was consulted by a woman suffering from panic attacks. She was at a time of crisis in her life. She had broken up with her partner in a row, repeating what had happened with her previous partner; her academic performance had been greatly affected, and she was on the verge of being expelled from her course. She had found herself a new boyfriend after the second break-up, who had asked her hand for marriage, to which she had agreed.

She wanted to settle down in life and find what had eluded her in recent years. One day, after an episode of food poisoning, she was given a serum intravenously, and her fiancé had to leave her in hospital in order to return to work. This was when her first panic attack occurred. She was somewhat settled in an initial consultation by naming the condition as "panic attacks" and decided to continue the treatment in order to prevent them happening again. From being in a state of complete chaos, she seemed to have found that speaking – "using her brain", as she called it – calmed her inner agitation. Close attention to the detailed account of her first experience of panic found certain elements that offered clues to her mode of being and her symptom. These elements included separation from the significant other (when her fiancé had to leave her in the hospital), failure in her university course, and her attempts to compensate for a loss or regain capacity in her daily life through analysis. There was, however, another element which added an important detail to her sense of limitation and restriction: the IV line attached to her forearm, which tied her to the hospital bed. Her body was symbolically restrained. The first set of elements that I have described point to a neurotic structure: a barred subject and a strategy of coping with the first loss or lack in the operation of alienation, and the passage from S1 to S2 in the operation of separation. However, the experience of the IV line seems to bear on events of the body: a jouissance located at a bodily level.

Coming to analysis was her first experience of a talking therapy and she was at first determined only to "get back on track", taking little interest in causes. But the more she spoke of the state of affairs in her life, her past history, her choice of men and friends, her family structure, etc., the more enjoyable she found this engagement in another aspect of speaking that involved a different way of questioning a fundamental aspect of her being.

At this point, cutting the sessions at certain moments of discontinuity in the signifying chain of her speech helped her shift position in speaking of her life. Her mode of storytelling changed and the cut made the unconscious manifest and enabled its gradual delivery in the consulting room. She became the subject of the unconscious in order to discover what she wanted to be beyond her way of relating to the Other's lack, as in being a partner or a daughter with certain characteristics. She tried to make sense of the symbolic lack in the Other and face her own lack as castration, while becoming less unsettled. She had become an analysand, in the sense that she had a strong desire to analyse rather than simply to rid herself of a dysfunctional symptom or to arrange a temporary fix. Besides therapeutic effects, some shifts of position became possible for her in life. The analytical act directed the work of analysis towards a different lack of being/wanting to become (manque-à-être). She continued her relationship with her husband while accepting some aspects of her previous position in a love relationship, which had involved locating and identifying with the Other's desire in the form of what he might need in life. She had a more meaningful relationship with her husband, constantly finding and inventing new ways of dealing with the sexual non-rapport as well as acknowledging that she did not want a child: her feminine position. This time, her positioning towards the Other's lack was not at the cost of self-sabotage or total sacrifice, as it had previously been.

She left the work twice because she needed to deal in her own time with an activation of the unconscious. In the first session after the first break, she said that she would have left the work much sooner if the direction of the treatment had been oriented only towards helping her to cope. She had managed to create a space for herself to face a hole in the Other and make something out of it for herself. In other words, the work was not simply between the Symbolic and Imaginary, but was geared to the Real of sexual non-rapport. If the work had, for example, only been concerned with searching for and discovering a fundamental phantasy such as "being stuck" (which was, indeed, her case), no radical shift in the core of her being (mode of being) would have happened. More importantly, her own agency was given a space to approach and interpret her fantasy, her symptom and her subjective position in language. It was only then that a change became possible for her. In fact, it was through recognising the agency of her body in dealing with jouissance in the hospital vignette that her narrative was pushed towards the desert of meaning: the rational and reality. I tried to speak to her body on that occasion, to her Real body, the body lying on a bed pinned down and drugged while the subject had felt left alone/behind in the hospital. This context had an unconscious interpretation of "death" in her personal history, an interpretation that was unavailable to her conscious mind early on in the work, but that emerged later, when she said that none of her first significant others had come out of hospital alive during her early childhood.

The second time she resumed analysis, the final shift happened. She had started to weave another symptom for herself, illustrated by a change of career. She was no longer reading the narrative around her being, but rather writing her symptom. She managed to rename the castle of psychoanalysis with a name proper to herself. She ceased to be a subject of the unconscious and instead became a "parlêtre", capable of dealing with a fundamental touch of the Real in the form of unnamed "jouissance" at the level of the body.

In the next chapters, I will say more about Lacan's ultimate legacy regarding the unconscious, based on the "parlêtre", Real body and "sinthome".

Topological representation of the subject

While Freud's proposed structure of the psyche features three distinct agencies based on the conflicts between inner perception and external reality, the Lacanian model of the transformable subject speaks through a topological trinity bearing an object – *objet a* – in the intersection of the topological rings of the Borromean knot. None of the rings works independently from the others. Freud's proposition in the second topic of a subjective agency associated with refusal, negation or contestation fails to explain the passage of a human infant to becoming an agent of his body – a body which enjoys independently – while at the same time figuring out his position in the Other's discourse by communicating with the first significant Other via the act of speech.

Lacan's reading of Freud's second topic tells us that the role played by the ego is not the principal role. Rather, power is given to the id. In the second topic, after almost 30 years' experience working with patients, as "sexed" and "social" beings, Freud had taken the crown from the ego and downgraded its role to that of a mediator, a middleman between the id and the super ego. Lacan pursued his reading of the id in his graph of desire, which functions at the level of the subject rather than that of the ego, and then, in his elaboration on the locus and role of the object of fantasy (in the id), which has the power to set desire in motion and to keep it alive. So, for Lacan, the Freudian subject is constituted through an interaction between the unconscious ego and the id.

Following Freudian thinking on the three operations of *deprivation, frustration* and *castration* in the primary mother–child fusion, Jean-Gerald Bursztein, a French analyst, explains that the essential pre-condition of a Borromean structure of the subject is a recognition of the absence of the mother, whereby the child feels an alteration of pleasure and displeasure or experiences frustration and then castration. The child who is invested on at the level of the mother's fantasy as the object of drive needs to be introduced to the subjective structure (the Borromean knot, representative of the subject) via the mother's discourse, which is subjected to a symbolic law beyond herself. Firstly, the loss of the voice allows the subject to relate to the Real via the Imaginary dimension of the gaze. Then, once the gaze is lost, the Symbolic dimension of the voice links the subject to the Real. The outcome is a topological representation of the subject who inherits a transmission of the structure from his mother's narratives. As a result, in the Real of the primary, fusional pleasure, which needs to be lost, the three dimensions of R, S and I include the *objet a* in their intersection and a subject is formed. The symbolic phallus is a substitute for the lost fusional pleasure and is the prerequisite for the subject to enter language. In neurosis, the Symbolic phallus is, in fact, a response to the mother's enigmatic desire and a force that closes the knot of being (Bursztein, 2016).

In psychosis, unlike in neurosis, the Borromean knot, as a topological representation of the subject, is not a closed braid. What has failed to occur is the passage beyond the captivating Imaginary gaze of the mother, and the apprehension of her as a lacking and deprived subject. In the search for an object that promises brilliance, the subject needs to take up a Symbolic position towards the phallus, but the psychotic subject does not submit to this need. The failure to take such a position earlier in life can make him the seeker for a compass in later life, a compass that can somehow compensate for his earlier refusal of a Symbolic lack in the Other. He will then be restricted to a static mode of jouissance; opting out of a journey with the support of a fantasy in relation to the phallus. Bursztein argues that, in the case of the non-psychotic subject, once the fusional pleasure between mother and child is lost, this lost pleasure is substituted by a subjective desire, an eroticised body – an appreciation of being alive that constitutes phallic jouissance. This jouissance, which is the accessible form of jouissance for each subject, has an echo in the fantasy – as the supportive scenario of the symptom. In other words, this lost fusional pleasure has an imprint in the symptom. However, in the case of psychosis, the primary jouissance which is not negativised and converted into desire and phallic jouissance jeopardises the sustainability of the subject's knot of being. In order to carry on living, his main focus in life may be finding a way to accommodate this excessive jouissance. Consequently, working through symbolisation with psychotic patients can potentially provide a structure to deal with the threat of chaos. Such a structure is, of course, not the same as the Symbolic structure, which is the result of the subject's own voluntary submission to the Symbolic law. Clinical work with the psychotic patient needs to focus on how to index the opaque Real, which a psychotic patient is unable to negativise due to an earlier failure of structure. The Symbolic can be made to penetrate the overwhelming state of being in the Real, creating room for the subject to move forward in life. None of this is to suggest that psychotics do not know how to enjoy themselves. On the contrary, they can be very attentive to life's beauties and able to indulge in fun and pleasure. Being alive, for the psychotic subject, may involve alternation between two extreme poles: an absolute loss of appetite for life, or, conversely, a radical indulgence in the full potential of any mode of enjoyment. Or, the lack of primary repression might mean that a psychotic subject has to deal with a constant dilemma around the meaning of being alive. A patient recounted to me how, one day in spring, the sun's rays had reflected off a mirror in her room and projected a rainbow onto the opposite wall. She said: "I know how to see the beauty of life; I know how to appreciate it for its beauty. I just don't know how to be accomplished at life". Being attentive to the cosmetic details of life is, indeed, in a real contrast with the problematic of the Other's desire in the neurotic who has submitted to phallic signification.

The fusional state between mother and child raises the question of the subject's space and distance from the Other. One of the main problems in schizophrenia is the subject's lack of tolerance and sense of urgency when it comes to dealing with the Other's demand. Maintaining a too-close or too-distant space between their and the Other is a common feature of this type of psychosis. To the psychotic subject, the only solutions in dealing with the Other are to become fused with it or to reject it altogether. Another approach for such a subject might be to create his own space around himself as compensation for an earlier positioning towards the Other whose lack was not registered. The psychotic subject will then raise his defensive wall as high as possible, in order to get a grip on reality in relation to others. Instead of appreciating or gaining satisfaction from being alive through phallic jouissance and desire, as in neurosis, the psychotic treats existence as a puzzle (how to exist?) or as a duty. He may either know exactly what he demands from a contract between him and the Other and what is due to both sides, or he may be in a state of utter confusion. His subjectivity operates in terms of "My room, my cell, my space", with a specific emphasis on the borders between inside and outside.

As regards choosing to remain in a fusional state with the first significant Other, a psychotic subject once told me that she was quite happy to be in relationship with herself. A prop is needed when the function of the three orders of R, S and I cannot be kept in place though the Borromean knot. To prevent the loose tie between them from unravelling, a plait has to be put in place, which is not the "point de capiton" (Lacan, 1955–6), but a bandage: the sinthome (Lacan, 1977–8). A reading of the Freudian second topic through the Lacanian Borromean knot suggests that, in psychosis, the phallus does not function as a strong binding between the three strands (R, S and I) that can plait a solid knot, thereby leading to the patient's need to invent a sinthome to keep the knot of the three registers together.

In the following two clinical cases, we will see how opting to remain in the primary fusion with the care giver can lead to a problematic relationship with the Other and the body later in life. When certain conditions are not met on the care giver's side – when, for example, the child is not invested as an object at the level of the maternal fantasy, or the thread of the Symbolic law is not safe enough to be followed, the jouissance is not properly introduced to the subject's body alongside the structure of the law, so that the dyadic, fusional state between the child and the first significant Other remains whole and without loss. In order to understand this, we should remember that the idea of a paradise – as an analogy for the phallus – is always associated with a "loss", an "absence" or a "minus". Therefore, a paradise, in order to be a workable concept, is always a "lost" paradise. In neurosis where the operation of repression has taken place, a longing for the lost paradise is echoed in the subject's desire and symptom. In psychosis, by contrast, where negation and foreclosure of a contract with the paternal metaphor have occurred, there is a claim – a claim, which is hard to maintain – for a safe place in paradise.

Case I

A young child had started to show seriously unsettled behaviour towards others at school. During a morning break in the timetable, she had turned all the other children's seats in the classroom in the direction opposite to hers. She had then started a fight with another child sitting next to her. When her teacher intervened, the girl's response was "I don't want anybody around me". She wanted to go home immediately. She did not go back to school for the rest of the year. At home, her elder sister was in the habit of giving her a daily report on her school day (they had only a year between them and went to the same school). She had a problematic and uneasy relationship with her mother, and only felt close to her sister. I wondered what was so special about her sister's position in her childhood. They had been constant playmates and her sister was her confidante. The sister was evidently far more trusted and less persecutory than the mother (the mother imposed strict rules within the family, which did not seem to have worked well for the younger sister), and the attachment to her sibling peer meant that she was still in fusion with the Other. However, this fusion with her sister was becoming a problem rather than a solution. There had been no effort to maintain distance and now, after years of an effortlessly dyadic relationship with only one peer, entering school was, for the younger sister, like leaving behind a life of freedom and entering a new and hostile environment, where new rules and a new social bond were imposed. The agency of the other was foreclosed and was interpreted as an imperative. A "social bond" between just two subjects is not a social bond in the proper sense; it is not a matter of learning "dos" and "don'ts", and the girl had re-experienced her original mark of foreclosure when – outside the nest, at school – she had to face the Other. Her reaction was to try creating a space – a literal one – for herself by moving chairs in the classroom in order to push away all her classmates. On another occasion, she had even said to her teacher, discussing her behaviour in the class: "So, you think that others have the right to dominate me, just because I'm smaller?" The size of her body had an abstract meaning for her. After a year of therapy, during which attendance at school remained difficult, she named her problem. She created some artwork and started to show it off to other children. She found she was good at sport and enjoyed the experience of winning. Through art and sport she found her own way of tackling her social anxiety. Having initially chosen to remain in a paradise-like fusion with her significant Other, she gradually coped with the possibility of a lack in the Other, which had not been inscribed as a Symbolic lack earlier in her life. The clinical work was oriented towards coming to term with a lost paradise.

Case II

When I first received Moe in my practice, he was in his late 30s. His intelligence and eloquence in the first consultation moved me to such an extent that I was puzzled why he was sitting in the patient's chair. There were no apparent signs of suffering as he reminisced about past events and made no complaints about his present life. Focusing on his adulthood, he spoke of a woman in his life, Jay, with whom he was apparently living, and with whom he engaged in daily activities. She sounded like a soulmate to him. Jay's presence had a pivotal role in all the plans and decisions that he told me of. He had decided to move country based mainly on Jay's circumstances. He had chosen his university course and career on her recommendations. Moe was excited when talking about the indicated intense love and care between them and he showed no passion except when speaking of Jay. When I asked his reasons for coming to psychoanalysis, he said that he had been feeling a bizarre sensation in his legs and that the sensation had appeared at around the same time that Jay had been diagnosed with cancer. Doctors called his condition "restless legs". Moe was nursing Jay through her treatment and it was on Jay's advice that he had sought psychoanalysis. After our meeting, on his way out, he noticed a drawing by a young child on my desk. I asked him whether he had a child himself and he replied that he had never had a relationship with a woman. Jay was Moe's mother and her death, just before Jay's 40th birthday and just a few months after our first meeting, was a catastrophe from which he never recovered, in the sense that he was never again the same man as he had been before Jay's death.

What it was that had made this subject decide to remain in a union, in a state of fusion, with his mother oriented the direction of treatment, at least in its early stages. His mother had not raised him as a single parent, but she had been in charge of him from the outset and at all times, as his father was not trusted by her to take any responsibility for the child. According to Moe, his father had let the family down, mainly financially, but also because of his temper, which had made it almost impossible for Moe and his siblings to approach him. Moe certainly had not become his mother's object of deprivation – the "Thing" – but nor had he registered her lack and submitted to a Symbolic castration. The mother's love and care had nurtured a form of identification, where the formation of the ego had been foundational in the birth of subject and the subject had no chance to escape the captivating gaze of the mOther, due to his refusal of castration. The Imaginary dimension of the gaze remained a pivotal element for the subject: it kept his subjectivity from disintegrating. Moe was not a divided subject who searched for the unknown object of his mother's desire. Was there a functional frustration coming from his mother? The failure to make a passage from the realm of the Imaginary towards some way of dealing with a Symbolic lack in the Other had forced Moe to opt for "remainia" jouissance, where he stayed in a union with the mother who was for him a non-divided Other. The subject's desire had not taken shape in a way that could lead him to discover some sort of compensation for the primary loss, and there was no unconscious attempt to seek for the lost object outside the care giver, that is there was a failure of the passage, whereby, in a neurotic structure, the loss of the object is accepted, so that it can be located or invested somewhere else in life.

Any echo of the primary loss – to be found in a love object, for example – was not an option for Moe. He was still in a relationship with his caregiver as his, almost literal, "saviour" from an "irresponsible and temperamental" father. The voice – apart from being the object of the invocatory drive – can potentially give (or not give) a Symbolic dimension to a fixated, dyadic relation between the subject and the Other. A child can accept this new object (the Symbolic voice) after giving up on the Imaginary gaze. For Freud, the operation of castration happens as soon as a subject recognises and accepts this transition, and the result is a divided subject – divided between language and jouissance (between the Symbolic and Real) – who is on a mission to find answers to the enigma of the Other's desire.

Most of the material discussed in the work with Moe was a manifestation of the drive and jouissance. The work with him also demonstrates the difference between the concept of a subject's desire and the competences of the ego. Following the Other's advice or copying his/her footsteps in life does not equate to a manifestation of desire, fuelled by phallic jouissance after the loss of the first, fusional jouissance. In psychosis, a subject can be left in an overwhelming state of jouissance, immersed in the fusional one with the unbarred Other. The clinic amply demonstrates that many psychotic subjects look for the care and attention of a mother-figure in their future partner or, conversely, look after their partner in a motherly or nurturing manner. This attitude may be the only pillar upholding a sexual non-rapport between the couple.

Moe easily became paranoid about what was happening around him and was quite narcissistic in his mode of being in relation to others. He was captivated in the Imaginary gaze, as defined by the Lacanian mirror phase. Such a gaze leads to a formation of the unconscious ego, which is narcissistic in its essence. Narcissism and paranoid thoughts are common features of schizophrenia.

In Moe's case, the mother had devoted her life to a cause: that of "saving my child". If her investment on her child had been subjected to a Symbolic law and had frustrated Moe's demands, thus creating a space for his desire, and if Moe himself had moved on from his pleasure of "remainia" (the union with his mother) and formed a phallic jouissance (echoed in wanting "to be" or "to have" such and such in life), the necessary passage from the captivating gaze to the voice could have taken place. Other subjects – unlike Moe, and more like the young girl described in the first case – develop an uneasy relationship with their caregiver. Tension is part and parcel of any dyadic union in the realm of the Imaginary. A union or fusional relation between the subject and his Other leaves no independent position for a subject to claim and take up.

Some concluding remarks on the subject of the unconscious

Where does the work of analysis terminate? Can one be sure that one will not continue to be surprised by unconscious knowledge? Why might some of us feel unwell again after the end of analysis? If the super-ego is conceptualised as derived from a specific culture and from family discourse, would the practice of psychoanalysis be possible trans-culturally? What is the source of the subject's agency in dealing with impositions?

When a subject's division is recalled at some point in his life and when the fixing point of his manque-à-être fails him, he might choose to search for the truth of his being through psychoanalysis. In a crisis the act of speaking – as a medium – might help him give an initial structure to an overwhelming state of jouissance, generated from a dysfunctional symptom (to be discussed in more detail later in this book). Such a structure can reduce the anguish which a subject experiences around the question of his being in a social bond, and it might only be after a crisis of anguish that a subject can become an explorer of his mode of being and his position in relation to the Other. There are moments in analysis that are felt but not necessarily articulated, which leave marks (lasting effects) on a subject. According to Lacan in his 11th Seminar, the analytical act should aim and push towards the earlier operation of "alienation", which came before a subject's separation from the Other. The unconscious does not belong to the past. Its irregular pulsation – as an opening and a closing-off – testifies to an a-temporality.

In the clinic, when such a pulsation occurs, the analyst, whose unconscious is worked through in another space, becomes attentive and intervenes. The field of the unconscious, which includes the subject, can remain beyond any symbolism. What distinguishes each particular subject from all the others is the way in which he relates to the unconscious knowledge of his being – how he comes to term with the primary jouissance to which he is born. When the union with the Other is lost, a space is potentially created and taken up by the subject of the unconscious.

The barred subject of the unconscious, with holes and inconsistency, comes into being as an effect of the mother tongue. The mother tongue, with a compact, autistic and ambiguous nature which is not the same as the spoken language of the care giver, needs to be introduced to the subject's body. In his later seminars, *Encore* and *Sinthome*, Lacan formulates and concludes his thoughts on the subject of the unconscious. He moves from the idea of a subject formed by the effect of language to a "being" marked by the tongue (the mother tongue) as a bodily event.

Towards the end of the analysis of one patient (a neurotic subject), the analysand spoke more and more in her mother tongue during the sessions. I did not know her mother tongue. However, I was able to intuit what was happening between us, as two "parlêtres", at the level of the unconscious. It was as if the analyst in her chair no longer existed for the analysand. There was no further symptom to be addressed to the Other of the unconscious and she was approaching closer to the operation of "alienation". It seemed to me that this phase of her analysis could be described as her golden ticket to the Chocolate Factory (evoking the children's film of that name), as she experienced the magic of "being" with less concern about divided subjectivity. Charlie Bucket (of *Chocolate Factory* fame) fully enjoys his experience of exploring the factory, satisfying drives at the level of his body through cheerful music, spoiling his taste buds, feasting on visual richness and, of course, moments of abstinence from what he has been told to avoid in order to guarantee the continuation of pleasure. At the end, he comes out of the Factory and back to his old life with his loving family, which he did not want to abandon. Fulfilling his subjective drive arrangement did not change the status of his symptom.

In an interview at a North American university in 1975, Lacan equates one possible end of analysis with being somehow "psychotic" (Lacan, 1975). It is, I think, possible to see the sense of this surprising suggestion. The testimony of the clinic suggests that the subject of the unconscious who is attentive to the Other's lack is full of stories of life missions, enjoys long narratives and intellectualisation of the act of speaking and eventually attains the jouissance of being. In other words, towards the end of an analysis, the neurotic subject, without actually becoming psychotic, attains a state that has some similarities with the clinic of psychosis: a more accessible form of jouissance, greater freedom in manifestation of the drive, less complaint of division and less identification with the Other's desire.

Bibliography

Bursztein, G. J. (2016). *The topological transformation of Freud's theory*. Marie-Laure Bromley-Davenport (Trans.). London: Karnak.

Freud, S. (1923). The Ego and the Id. In: J. Strachey, ed., *The standard edition of the complete psychological works of Sigmund Freud, vol. XIX*. London: Vintage, 2001, pp. 3–63.

Harari, R. (2004). *Lacan's four fundamental concepts of Psychoanalysis*. Judith Filc (Trans.). New York: Other Press.

Lacan, J. (1953–4). *The seminar of Jacques Lacan: Book 1: Freud's papers on technique*. John Forrester (Trans.). New York and London: Norton.

Lacan, J. (1954–5). *The seminar of Jacques Lacan: Book II: The Ego in Freud's theory and in the technique of Psychoanalysis*. John Forrester (Trans.). New York and London: Norton.

Lacan, J. (1955–6). *The seminar of Jacques Lacan: Book III. The Psychoses*. J.-A. Miller, ed., and Russell Grigg (Trans.). London: Routledge, 1993.

Lacan, J. (1956–7). *Le séminaire de Jacques Lacan. Book IV: La relation d'objet*. Paris: Seuil, 1994.

Lacan, J. (1963–4). *The seminar of Jacques Lacan: Book XI: The four fundamental concepts of psychoanalysis*. Alan Sheridan (Trans.). New York and London: Norton.

Lacan, J. (1975). Conférences et entretiens dans des universités nord-américaines. In: *Scilicet No 6/7*. Paris: Seuil, 1976, p. 42.

Lacan, J. (1975–6). *Le séminaire livre XXIII: Le sinthome*. Paris: Seuil.

Lacan, J. (1977–8). *Le séminaire livre XXV: Le moment de conclure*. Unpublished Manuscript.

Figure 2.1 Eleven Minus One, photograph by Bardia Moeini

Chapter 2

Symptom formation

Introduction

When I think of my mother tongue, poetry is the first, immediate form in which it comes to mind. In fact, I cannot think of the Persian language without thinking of poetry. Once, out of curiosity, I picked up a book of poems by Hafez translated into English. I could not associate the lines of the translation with the original verse in the poem. It is, of course, common knowledge that the translation of poetry is a difficult task. Success in preserving certain characteristics of the original text usually depends on a basic, primary interpretation by the translator. In some cases, the addition of certain aesthetic twists makes it possible for the translator to keep the complexities of the original verse almost intact. The example of poetry translation helps to understand how unconscious interpretation from an equivocal mother tongue can operate. The subject of the unconscious attempts to decode the opacity of the primary jouissance into which he is born in order to make meaning of his being in language – to make signification. The subject forms the core of his symptom based on this initial interpretation. The symptom (after being formed) indexes and translates the Real, thus offering the subject a mode of jouissance (Morel, 2019).

Being well versed in Persian poetry, my attempt to read a Persian poem in English translation made me realise that it was not the meaning of the original poem that generated my enjoyment. What induced excitement in me was the sound of the words and the rhythm or movement hidden in each verse. It was nothing to do with how we think or analyse upon hearing a piece of literature; it was, rather, an unconscious effect or mark produced by the verses as one style of narration in my mother tongue. When reading Persian poetry, I seemed to experience a form of jouissance which Lacan termed the "Other jouissance": an excitement beyond any that words can describe, a form of enjoyment which alleviates the painful encounter with the impossible Real while generating a motivating pleasure. In the Lacanian Borromean knot, the Other jouissance is situated between the Imaginary (understanding the meaning of the poem's verses) and Real (excitement induced by the rhythm of the poem). Such a modality of jouissance is experienced at the level of the body. I could never become a poet in my mother tongue. I do not

DOI: 10.4324/9781003184799-3

possess the talent, skill and desire to do so. Unlike phallic jouissance, which fuels a subject's desire, the Other jouissance offers the subject a certain liberation and arises from any structure of language. We will discuss this concept later, in more detail in the chapter on the Real body.

In this chapter, we will explore the concept of symptom formation in more depth in Lacan's work by referring to some cultural and clinical examples.

A purpose in life

The psychoanalytic unconscious, which differs from any unconscious that has been developed in philosophy, offers one particular reality or truth to each subject. However, the nature of unconscious reality for each subject is intertwined with the unconscious reality of the Other due to the nature of language. Unconscious interpretation, the formation of a symptom and of desire, and the arrangement of the drive are all influenced by language and happen as a result of a transaction with the Other. For these reasons, we cannot establish strict borders that separate our reality and dreams from the Other.

Lacan's teaching moves away from the Symbolic to the Real; his concepts of the 1950s, that the subject starts from the mirror phase and that the symptom is a signifier, lead to the concepts of parlêtre and the sinthome. In Lacan's later work, the concept of the subject is that of a subject doomed to speak. The subject is a being which is represented as a knot (Borromean) that remains sustainable thanks to a sinthome: the fourth ring in the knot (Lacan, 1975–76). The mother tongue or maternal/primary jouissance is the fabric of the Real from which a symptom is formed. The symptom in the realm of the Real originates from the initial subjective interpretation from the equivocal mother tongue, and the paternal metaphor is then used by the subject to finalise the status of the symptom (Morel, 2019). The symptom ultimately separates the subject from the mother and gives him a purpose for living, although a time may come when it no longer succeeds in doing this. The symptom translates a mode of jouissance in the Real for each subject. Psychoanalysis is one possible way to question the status of the symptom, to challenge its function and to modify or alter it in order to perform the task of translation differently. In the Borromean knot the symptom is situated in the realm of the Real.

Now, if the symptom is not formed by a subject, there is nothing to play the essential role, which it plays, and the subject is doomed to remain stuck in a constant equivocation in the mother tongue. If, in neurosis, interpreting the maternal equivocation (besides the operation of the Father, which names the jouissance) can help a subject construct a symptom, as a separating agent, in psychosis; on the other hand, the subject remains stuck in the domain of equivocations of the mother tongue. He was never able to leave the mother tongue matrix, with its ambiguous nature. Such ambiguity, which extends over the three domains of meaning, libido and the Other, will then affect the psychotic subject's mode of being. In some cases of psychosis, a single, rigid meaning, made from the equivocal narrative of the care giver, has replaced the function of the symptom and consequently, overshadows the subject's being. Such a morbid construction can be present in a subject's reality like a sword of Damocles over his head, or as if he was born under a curse: he is wicked!

In analysis, basing ourselves on this theorisation, we hope that the subject will eventually construct his own "artwork" as a sinthome, thereby reducing his suffering as a speaking being. The sinthome becomes not just a *translator* of jouissance in the Real but also a *writer*. It creates and generates anew (like a writer) a bearable mode of jouissance for a parlêtre so that the pain of being becomes liveable and the personal myth which was present at the beginning of the treatment is no longer needed. Over the course of analysis, we move from a symptom (translator only) to a sinthome (writer and translator). We arrive at an irreducible mode of being, a parlêtre: a speaking being marked by properties of language other than the single narrative of the mother tongue.

The later conceptualisation of the subject and the symptom in Lacanian theory concerns both the mode of interpretation and the direction of the treatment in the clinic of neurosis and psychosis. We will approach these questions in clinical vignettes later in this chapter. The question to ask is how, in the course of an analysis, we can move towards the reduction of a personal myth/family drama in a suffering subject (who suffers from his symptom) and allow him weave a new mode of being in the domain of language, a mode of being that is sustainable with the help of a sinthome?

Instead of employing clinical interpretations, which aim to reconstruct the story behind each symptom, based on personal history, we suggest an alternative approach: deconstructing the primordial interpretation, formed by the subject of the unconscious in relation to the equivocation found in his mother tongue. In other words, we need to find a way of moving in the reverse direction, towards the earlier unconscious operation of equivocation and signification, and to decompose the primary signification by means of equivocal interpretation.

We use equivocal interpretation as an analytical act in different ways in the clinic of psychoanalysis in order to help the subject avoid being fooled by his personal myth, which may be the cause of his malaise. In some cases, it is possible to arrive at one significant, equivocal, maternal narrative, upon which a myth around the subject's being has been built. If the analyst's interpretations in the course of the sessions aiming only at constructing yet another myth around his narratives, this would prevent the subject from moving towards the primordial, unconscious operation of interpretation (the signification), based on which a symptom has come into being. Such an approach makes the analyst a storyteller, who creates a new myth or narrative for the subject, but never allows the subject to construct his own knot of being anew. The outcome is a hall of mirrors reflecting endless interpretations, with no meaningful effect on the subject's life. He will not feel that he is telling his own story. Such an approach to interpretation might offer some therapeutic effects, but certainly not at the level of the symptom, which has to be formed by the subject's own agency.

In order to help an analysand to create a different medium, through which he would be able to continue enjoying life, the earlier construction of the symptom, which is presented to the analyst at the outset as a source of malaise and discomfort, needs to be demolished. Equivocation is used in order to tackle the rigid construction of the symptom, encouraging its replacement by a sinthome, which involves less trouble for the analysand. As psychoanalysts, we create a space that allows a touch of the Real to brush the subject of the unconscious. This could be one of the reasons why the process of analysis sometimes produces uncanny experiences, and why it takes so long. The analysand has to prepare to go through an alienating experience of not being (désêtre). In the clinic of psychosis, where there is no symptom in place, the process of psychoanalysis supports the subject in constructing a sinthome as a supportive ring that can bind the three registers (Real, Symbolic and Imaginary) together. The aim of analytical work with psychosis would then be how to form this "fourth" ring.

In the next section, we will use an example from cinema to elaborate the work of equivocation and signification which, according to Lacan's early teaching, are the unconscious operations used by the subject to fashion a symptom. These operations are where we see the agency of each subject. Psychoanalysis rejects the emphasis which is often placed today on the supremacy of given, factual knowledge from an all-knowing position as the key to assuring people's well-being. In psychoanalysis the agency of each subject in forming a symptom is recognised and the subject is given space to choose how to enhance their mode of living. Instead of blaming external circumstances for a subject's suffering, psychoanalysis elaborates the subject's choices based on his ethical stance. This is not to deny that the narrative into which a subject is born, socio-economic factors or family structure (if any) play a role in forming a particular mode of being. But psychoanalysis sees all those factors through the lens of the subject. The important question is: How does he grant the Other's input to his mode of being? So the analyst helps the subject re-write his narrative by promoting the impact of subjective agency on external circumstances, based on the subject's ethical stance between language and jouissance.

Inception: equivocation and signification

The film *Inception* (2010) by Christopher Nolan explores the theme of dream and reality. The story involves the use of an advanced technology to infiltrate a person's sleeping mind and extract valuable information by sharing a dream with them. The world of the dream in the film is a creative state of architectural construction, while the world of reality follows a linear plot where the protagonist (a professional in the use of the advanced dream technology) has a criminal record that prevents him from being reunited with his children. A businessman agrees to arrange for the record to be quashed if the protagonist (by the name of Cobb) will use his method in reverse, planting in the mind of the son of an ageing rival the idea of dissolving his father's business empire (this planting is the "inception", as opposed to Cobb's usual business of "extraction"). The inception is to be carried out through a shared dream that Cobb and his team have with the target and involves manipulating the images and words of a particular scene that the target had with his father in his childhood. Based on this new (manipulated) reality, the targeted subject will place a different and new interpretation on his value for the Other and make a decision that favours the business of Cobb's employer without having any conscious knowledge of the conspiracy that has led him to do this.

We might alter the story slightly for our purposes. Instead of an idea being planted in the subject's head by outsiders, let us suppose that it was subject himself, as agent, who formed a new interpretation upon encountering a different account of his childhood reality. The original interpretation had given a meaning to the subject's being in the domain of language, acting as the foundation on which the subject begins his journey in life. The son of the conglomerate owner had interpreted a childhood vignette and formed a meaning for himself. This fundamental meaning had played a central role in his life, in what he was and what he was supposed to do in his professional life. He wanted to inherit his father's role as head of the conglomerate. In doing so, he assumed that this is what his father would have wanted, and that his father would have been proud of him. On this interpretation, being a subject who is wanted and loved by the Other meant being a strong and capable leader of his father's legacy. Such a position in the language would make his existence for the Other meaningful. After being confronted with a different aspect of reality, his new interpretation of his being for the Other meant that he can be something else and yet still enjoy and appreciate his being. Now, he was willing to continue his own chosen path in life without being at the mercy of guilt (repaying an assumed debt for his father). A different subjective interpretation sets him off in a whole different direction in life. As if the initial interpretation, which had constituted the very core of his symptom (being a successful leader of his father's company), was challenged later in life (although differently, in our version, from how it was challenged in the film plot, by "inception" or manipulation from outside). It is not unusual in the clinic of psychoanalysis to see analysands find another way of living after recognising the identification between their desire and the desire of the Other, an identification that was shaped by a primary interpretation of the Other's lack. After this recognition, the jouissance is set free and the subject of the unconscious can work through it anew to form a different way to access enjoyment via a new purpose in life.

Some might read the film scenario based on a dyadic theme between dream and reality and others might argue that manipulating a perceived reality can decide a subject's destiny (as echoed in the way stoicism has been interpreted and used in some therapeutic approaches, such as CBT). We are suggesting an alternative reading of this excellent film, as showing us the birth of the subject of the unconscious. A subject carves a space for himself in the language and the narrative he is born to. Then it is for his own agency to form (or not form) a symptom, a symptom which both separates his being from the Other and offers him enjoyment in life. The symptom is the journey each subject chooses in life, which can be altered or modified later, as happened for the son of the businessman in *Inception*. After the "inception" the subject forms a new interpretation, based on which his new symptom or way in life burgeons.

In psychoanalysis, once a symptom ceases to offer an accessible mode of enjoyment to a subject, the journey of extensive elaboration of different aspects of subjective reality may begin. The reality of the subject is challenged and altered. After much detailed elaboration of a subject's primary unconscious interpretation, a new symptom can be fashioned, offering a new narrative in life for the subject. After some light has been shed on a hidden aspect of the subjective reality, it would be up to the subject of the unconscious how he perceives, interprets, accepts or rejects the truth of his being in language. Sometimes an analysand might get to the initial "inception" (primary interpretation), from which he had formed the core of his symptom, but decide that he wants to continue the same way of life rather than making a change, and the subject might suffer less in the light of the new unconscious knowledge, which he has gained. The subject is both the architect and manipulator of his unconscious reality.

In Nolan's film, the end of the subjective adventure is well depicted in the final scene where distinguishing dream and reality does not matter anymore. Cobb runs to play with his children, with whom he was so desperate to be reunited. This was his cornerstone/symptom in life.

In the next section, we turn to the clinic of psychoanalysis to pinpoint the subject's agency in forming and supporting his mode of being from the fabric of Real.

A case of neurosis and the mother tongue

An analysand began analysis as treatment for her anorexia. After an initial assessment of her condition, I noticed that she had suffered at least three episodes of recurring physical illness at eight-year intervals, all, unsurprisingly, related to her digestive system and all leading to surgical intervention. Her anorexia was not severe, and she said that it was, to an extent, manageable. However, she wanted to know the cause of her problem. I drew attention to the number 8 in her narrative and she came up with a series of associations in her family history, regarding as her own age and certain life events around that age. However, none of the associations moved her unconscious. Rather than encouraging her endeavours to construct a myth around her symptomology, I encouraged her to a close reading of her symptom through a series of equivocal interpretations. Taking her first presentation of herself seriously, that is, that she was ill and suffering the effects of avoiding food, I singled out a signifier, not reducible to any further meaning, which was the number 8.

She told me that she was happily married with a husband who was supportive throughout her hospital treatments. Putting aside any analysis of her husband's symptom, she was, effectively, being loved by being taken care of. Without assuming knowledge or framing hypotheses about her difficult symptom, and avoiding any collusion with the translation carried out by the symptom into the Real of bodily illness, we landed upon the word for the number 8 in Persian, which was her mother tongue. The number 8 is written in Persian in a form that represents a tent, a temporary refuge or even a space to rest. Following my intervention, she remembered her father's hospitalisation due to a bowel problem when she was four years old. The number of the hospital room was eight, a fact that she remembered because her mother, who was already separated from her father at the time, had shown her the number on the room door and said: "Look, this is a tent where your father is staying for a short while". The equivocation of "staying for a while" was interpreted into the symptom of suffering from illnesses of the bowel herself and needing surgery to remain alive, which recurred every eight years. The meaning taken from early life had given her a symptom that translated her father's illness into her own bowel illness. Moreover, her father had to go through several episodes of fasting before going into surgery. This had been the first and only time she had been seen a solution to the impossible relationship between her parents: her mother, despite their divorce, had nursed her father in the hospital, just as my analysand's husband was doing for her. The work of analysis progressed, allowing her to construct a different sinthome to support her subjective knot. She no longer had to remain a patient nursed by her partner and seek jouissance from her bodily illnesses, focused mainly on her digestive system.

We push towards the enigma in the analysand's narrative – that which is most foreign to him or her – in order to have an impact on the subject of the unconscious. Such an effect in the Real enables the construction of a new medium, with which a subject can gain independence from the imposed law of language, by tying a new knot of being. In the case just described, she no longer remains caught up in somatic illness. This new medium is the sinthome. We do not adhere to any governing methodology in the clinic of psychoanalysis, except that knowing how and what *not to interpret* in order to leave an effect at the level of the symptom's status. The act of interpretation is not the same as decoding the pattern of a symptom. The interpretation is supposed to target a subjective agency over forming a symptom; a symptom which serves a specific function for the subject's position in the language. At the end of the treatment, a subject is not the same as when he or she entered the analysis at the beginning. In particular the analyst should no longer exists as an Other.

A case of psychosis and the mother tongue

When I began working with K, she was in the midst of a family crisis involving aggression between family members. Her own involvement in the situation – as main participant and cause of the family quarrel – had triggered an act of aggression on her side leading to a psychotic episode and the reappearance of self-harming, which had a long history in her case. She had struck her sibling and seen blood on his nose, ran away from the scene and started to cut her arms and legs. According to her, she did this in order to induce *pain* and *blood* on her body. At our first meeting, she said that she had a tremendous fear that she had actually become what her mother had always called her: *a monster*. She had been beaten by her mother with no intervention from social services. Her first interpretation of her mother's cruelty was in relation to her physical size. She was the tallest and biggest child of the family. Hence, self-cutting on her arms and legs seemed to be an attempt to shorten her arms and legs. She had been told, later in life, that her mother had several times mentioned that having a daughter *destroys* a mother's life: K's mother's history with her own mother was very much relevant to her own maternal position towards K. Working through K's interpretation from her mother's narrative, the significance of *blood* was associated with her mother's blood in her veins, from which she wanted to escape. Her interpretation from her mother's narrative of being a "monstrous" girl who destroyed her mother's life had overshadowed her whole being. She was captivated in this particular interpretation and the meaning of her being was reduced to what to do or not to do in order to be that horrifying image. Consequently, she was paralysed in her social and personal life, unable to do anything with her talent and education. Through the work, she gradually became able to escape the abusive mother who swamped her, and to produce a different way of working with her primary signification. Her mental and physical being were interpreted differently thanks to her new sinthome, which was to undertake a course of study, following in her father's footsteps. For her, the father was a literal saviour. She had always had identified with her father in relation to her mother. She believed that her father was also a victim of her mother' cruelty. In K's case, the work of analysis was conducted in a language different from her mother tongue, creating a safe space in which to explore her new mode of being.

The art of knots

From an analytical perspective the transmission of elements in the narrative of the previous generation to a subject's symptom is a highly complicated phenomenon. The subject has agency to tie a new knot from the original fabric which is his mother tongue. We will conclude our argument by treating the fabric of the mother tongue as a fundamental fabric on which we tie the knot of our being, by referring (logically enough) to the art of carpet making.

Researching the history and philosophy behind the knotting of Persian rugs, I came to understand that the sketched pattern from which each rug is created originates from regional myths. The symbols that appear on a rug are interpreted both individually and collectively. They offer a meaningful story behind a pattern. However, they also represent the cultural elements of a group of people that are passed down from generation to generation. Besides the learning of traditional knowledge, there is another element in such a mode of transmission of artisanal skill from mother-women of one generation to those of the next. It is an element that is also found in the Real effect of a mother tongue in symptom formation in neurosis or, potentially, in forming a life compass in psychosis. Knotting a better rug, adding a twist, changing a business model in an artisan business or, in other words, becoming a better version of the previous generation occurs on the basis on an original material/fabric, in which our parents' symptom resonated. We add, correct, enhance or introduce some new twists to the original symptom. This is what psychoanalysis is interested in and where its concern lies, unlike many other fields of human science, from philosophy to sociology. In analysis, we do not reduce the function of the skilled work of an artisan-mother to an operation of the *paternal metaphor* at the level of the mother's desire. It can also condition the child's own decision to form their knot of being, telling their own story through their symptom.

The pattern on the rug has come to be as the result of thousands of knots being tied to a set of background vertical strings, making them sit next to each other. There is a wide variety of knots, depending on how they are tied in the different regions of the world where rugs are made. The identity, value and effect that each type of rug offers depends on how these knots tie the fabric to the background strings, to allow the intended sketch or story to appear. Without the support of knots firmly fastened and tied to these background strings, the rug does not exist; in a similar way, nor does our mode of being. The background strings can act as an appropriate analogy for the position of the mother tongue, as a fabric in the Real that contains no Symbolic law. A subject might choose to remain a weakly tied knot, as is the case in psychosis. The loose knot of being can be more securely fastened with the help of the sinthome as the fourth ring, while in neurosis a knot is already firmly fastened by the object *a* and conditioned by the symptom. The symptom can be modified or changed if it is generating too much suffering for a subject. What has been a *reading/reciting* of a myth gives way to the act of *writing* what we might term "poetry", employing other properties of the language in order to remain as a sustainable knot. The subject now knows how to deal with his life. He plays his game differently from how he did the past, in the limited window of agency that he possesses in the face of the imposing law of language. A subject may come close, in certain situations in life, to the primary jouissance, from which he once managed to escape. Through analysis, he can use his new narrative to deal with such situations, from a different position and well supported by his sinthome.

From reciting a historical myth to the hearing of sounds that are specific to each one of us, this is a journey we have decided to travel when we knock on the analyst's door. The verses of Omar Khayyam are expressive of the Lacanian concept of parlêtre and sinthome that may come into play towards the end of an analysis:

> The secrets of eternity neither you know, nor I; and of this enigmatic letter, neither you read, nor I.
> Behind the curtain there is the talk of you and I; when it falls shall neither you remain, nor I

The end of analysis is where the secret of the Real touches our being without any need for further interpretation. This is manifest in the first line of Khayyam's poem, while the second line can be linked to a full/fool narrative that we have formed around us at the beginning of the treatment, a narrative that leaves out the subject and deals only with being. It is the art of a subject in analysis to bring out a new narrative analogous to poetry, which is outside any trans-generational narrative, but is inspired and influenced by it.

Bibliography

Lacan, J. (1975–6). *Le séminaire livre XXIII: Le sinthome*. Paris: Seuil.
Morel, G. (2019). *The law of the mother: An essay on the sexual sinthome*. Lindsay Watson (Trans.). London: Routledge.

Figure 3.1 The Extimacy, photograph by Bardia Moeini

Chapter 3

Subjectivity and fairy tales

Introduction

From "once upon a time" to "happily ever after", from the past to the future, every fairy tale holds out the promise of eternal happiness. We fashion dreams, fantasies or even central goals in our lives from fantastical folktales that have been told to us. We identify with certain characters in fairy tales and feel strong antipathy towards others. In the late nineteenth century, Freud took the idea of fantasies and the concoction of myths seriously, so much so that a new cultural product – psychoanalysis – was invented as a tool to address the fundamental question: *What are we?*

We might have enjoyed the storyline, characters or the setting of a particular fairy tale. We might have disliked the logic of the storyline, or conversely, adopted it. We might even have lived with the characters of fairy tales for quite some time in our childhood, if not well into adult life. Each of us might have plumped for one or more favourite tales, based on the personal myth we have created of our own being in language. Fairy tales arose from the folkloric narratives of each culture over many, many years, and travelled down the generations, gathering various time-bound features as they went. These culture-specific elements – found in each fairy tale – can leave a mark on a subject of the unconscious. They might even add a new set of specifications to the object of phantasy or define its general character, based on how they are narrated in each culture. The pattern of fairy tales remains transculturally the same in principle. All of them seem to promote a single motto or moral message: the victory of light over darkness. However, beyond the superficially dyadic theme – between the two extreme poles, the narrative arc of each tale contains successive moments of loss, despair and sorrow, transformed into an ideal state of serenity, which having been attained, of course, the story always ends. We are told only that life will continue just as it was at the moment of that happy ending. This is, in fact, a common fantasy heard in the psychoanalytic clinic, and it generates a specific mode of jouissance for each subject of the unconscious. Such a fantasy is an echo of the wish to halt the passage of time at the moment when things promise to continue "happily ever after", a mark of the desire to freeze and hold that special, serene moment. This is not about

DOI: 10.4324/9781003184799-4

terminating or quashing something. On the contrary, it is an urge to make that precise moment endure eternally and continuously.

An essential element of all fairy tales, without which they are not proper fairy tales, is magic. The characters are made to suffer, wait patiently or fight, until the point at which they are either doomed or rescued by the power of magic. The magic in question is not illusion or a "superpower" that acts to effect change. It is the most anticipated moment in the story, the moment when both the main character and the reader are awestruck. The excitement induced for a subject by the power of magic goes beyond an illusion of success and victory, as understood in the domain of the Lacanian Imaginary and Symbolic. Such excitement comes into existence in the absence of these things. It only manifests in the Real in the form of anxiety induced from the mixture of anticipation and that fairy tales can provoke.

Magic and illusion in show-business – staging and playing out the impossible, disappearing and then re-appearing objects and people – are a way of creating an excitement that is also fascination, anguish or, perhaps, fear. Such feelings are experienced during the prolonged state of suspension and anticipation, until the moment when things are remade back into whatever they were before the magician's first intervention. In fact, this final act of re-appearing things is not what we call magic. Magic is what is experienced in the form of a Real, manifested as the experiencing of various emotions (affects) by an audience. This is what attracts people to such performances. Through the act of staging magic or through a fairy tale, anticipation and uncertainty generate an enjoyable excitement in the subject. Knowing the tricks behind an illusion can be disastrous for a display of magic: it kills the joy. Similarly, the secret of the magical power of a fairy tale hero or heroine is never explained. Sometimes it is not even revealed to the character themselves: They are born with it or invested with it unbeknown to them. This type of uncertainty is different from a subject's uncertainty about his/her mode of being. The latter generates anguish, from which a subject wants to escape, as if his knot of being was at risk of unravelling. Such uncertainly can arise from various causes. It can be the repetition of a situation where a subject feels entangled in primary jouissance, facing the Real of mortality, and when all his attempts to defend his subjective position fail (as in the failure of a symptom). Else, it can be a confrontation with the Real of sexuality without the trick of the drive.

How can we use the fabric of fairy tales, magic and staging to approach the question of subjectivity from a psychoanalytic perspective?

Mother tongue and fairy tale

The impact of fairy tales on children certainly goes beyond the absorbing of moral messages through decoding and interpreting a plot. Fairy tales do not merely help to imprint a form of social identity on a subject. Even in the act of copying the positions of fairy-tale characters, as sometimes happens in psychosis, there is always a subjective agency at work, deciding whether to follow or to defy. A fairy tale can be used as a fabric to concoct a personal myth during the formation of the subject. Fascination with (excitement by) fairy tales defeats any attempt at symbolisation.

Let us approach the impact of fairy tales on a subject using the Lacanian model of subjectivity and the R(eal), S(ymbolic) and I(maginary) interrelationship (Lacan, 1974–75). From the fabric of a fairy tale in the Real language (the mother tongue), the following three trends can be inferred:

1   The story line might offer room for a subject to fantasise and take up a social role/identity, which can be reformed or reshaped later in life. This is what can be referred to as the Imaginary ego. The very first foundations of a structure are introduced to the subject's psychical life through the divided theme of the fairy tale's plot: light and darkness, or good and evil. Depending on which subjective position he takes up in relation to the Symbolic law (the consequences of the character's actions, as implied by the plot of the fairy tale), a moral lesson can be drawn and form the Freudian superego. So the ethical stance of a subject can be influenced and shaped by those consequences.

2   A personal myth can be concocted from certain elements in a fairy tale, as a subjective, unconscious fantasy. A fantasy, being a support of the subject's symptom, is the scenario through which the subject moves towards the *object*. The movement towards the object of fantasy generates an accessible mode of jouissance (phallic jouissance) for the subject, constituting his "liveliness" and making it meaningful. This is possible when a subject has submitted to the Symbolic law of language, as is the case in neurosis. Later in this chapter, we will examine in more detail the meaning and importance of the question of psychical structures.

3   There is also a mode of excitement experienced by a subject in the form of fascination with the staging of the fairy tale, its "mise-en-scène", which will remain outside any meaning and structure. This excitement, as a bodily event, can be understood as another modality of jouissance. This other form of jouissance (Other jouissance) will be elaborated later in the book. Its enjoyment is offered to each subject through the arrangement of the drive. It can be manifested, at the level of drive, in a person's fascination with certain hobbies or the pursuit of a career in performance, cinema, theatre or some other form of show business. A subject needs to deal with his body as the first Other before fully acquiring his mother tongue with its equivocal nature (the Other of language). So the subject has to figure out two fundamental positions for himself as a speaking being: Firstly, towards the Other of the *body*, which seeks pleasure independently from the subject of the unconscious; and, secondly, towards the Other of *language*, through which a desire can (or cannot) be formed.

Neurosis and bedtime fairy tales

When a human baby is born into a discourse and wants to claim a position for himself in the domain of language, there are certain unconscious operations involved, and it is through such operations that the subject's agency manifests itself. In order to make meaning of our being in language, we attempt to understand what the Other demands from us and what they might lack. The Other's demand correlates with the subject's drive arrangement, and recognition of the Other's lack is linked with the formation of a desire. So this guess work (subjective interpretation) in the field of the mother tongue involves a montage of the drive, at the level of our body, and the creation of a meaning or mission in life in the form of a subject's desire. The spoken word, as a learned skill with language, is like a rope which a subject has acquired and used in order to climb out of a mute state of being. He has to pull his way out of an ambiguity by a rope which we call the operation of *signification* in psychoanalysis. A child might understand his care giver's demand but still refuse to speak for a time – if not forever, as the act of speaking is not the same as that of understanding. For each subject, that breakthrough moment lies in waiting: it is the moment when they move beyond simple sounds as an effort to communicate with others and pronounce their first words. A child might, however, opt to continue communicating only with sounds or by the use of a very few words, as happens with autistic children. Parents are almost always excited when the child says his first word(s). It is a magical and long anticipated moment.

Meanings occupy only a minimal part of the domain of language. Humans are not merely programmed to learn linguistic competence (correct matches between words and things) in their mother tongue. That is why, in the clinic of neurosis, interpretation at the level of meaning produces nothing of *lalangue* (the Lacanian term for the language in which the unconscious is represented) for a subject. As well as learning meanings, the subject also learns about the law of the Other's desire through what appears in their language, based on guesswork and assumptions about the object of the Other's desire, on the basis of which he shapes his own desire. This involves recognising a Symbolic position in relation to the Other's lack. And, even before the ability to speak is acquired, the child's body (Lacan tells us that the body image is initially recognised in the mirror phase) is invisibly marked by another aspect of language, beyond simple naming of different parts of the body or (perhaps) adding some complementary descriptions to them. This aspect of language and its effects on the body escape the limits of the Symbolic. As a consequence of Freudian castration or as a consequence of recognising a Symbolic lack in the Other (Lacan's formulation), the divided subject strives to find a sort of solution – through a *symptom* – for his mode of being, while taking pleasure from being alive (phallic jouissance).

What has just been outlined is, in fact, a neurotic subject's stance towards the Other of language and the body. If the symptom fails the subject – fails to provide him with a viable mode of enjoyment – it is through analysing different layers and properties of language that a new symptom (or "sinthome" in Lacan's terminology) can potentially be formed. The conduct of a psychoanalysis relies on equivocal intervention and interpretation in order to allow the subject of the unconscious to form a new way of living (Lacan, 1975–76). Let us now turn to clinical vignettes in order to understand this better.

To have a moving castle: a case of neurosis

An analysand once recounted that seeing the animated film *Howl's Moving Castle* made in 2005 had reminded him of a tale from folklore, which had obsessed him in early childhood. The tale and the plot of the film did not coincide exactly; but, from the film, he was able to pin down the pattern of his symptom as wanting to be constantly on the move from one place to another. Moreover, he saw a possible identification between the film protagonist and himself. At this stage of his analysis, he was elaborating his earliest connections with the external world and spoke of his bedtime rituals as a young child. His mother used to tell him stories or read him fairy tales.

At the beginning of the analysis, he was convinced that he wanted to settle down in one place, and it was only due to external circumstances that he was not able to fulfil his desire. He then tried to explore what it was that drove him to leave one place for another? How was the new destination chosen? These questions were posed to him. When more details of his symptom formulated as *moving* were explored, he realised that the decisions he made were oriented around a motif of restoring things to a better state or to an earlier time (like the wizard in his childhood fairy tale), as if he wanted to move backwards in time through the act of restoring things to an earlier state, which he always assumed to be a better state. This tendency was echoed in his unconscious strategy of prolonging and delaying tasks in his life. He was working in a scientific lab on a project oriented to enhancing and making improvements in people's life quality, and he had a tendency to be late in completing the tasks that were assigned to him there. In his relationships with women, he was often accused of being a *cold* and *distant* partner and of prioritising his work life over the relationship. Acknowledging his constant moving as a symptomatic pattern, he started to scrutinise the theme of restoring things to a better state or (as he also saw it) obstructing the passage of time. It took him almost two years from the first intervention to read what was written in his symptom and his subjective position towards the Other. He described himself as a quiet and private man who preferred to interact with his love partners from a *safe distance*, meaning that he could only keep up a relationship so long as there was not a demand for long-term commitment. But, although he found it difficult to commit to a relationship, it was essential for him to have a significant role in improving his partner's life. As he put it: he wanted to see them express pleasure at this improvement. To him, the idea of changing someone else's life was equated with having a *magical power*. His role in a love relationship was only meaningful for him as long as he was certain of having and deploying such "magic". Interpretations in the analysis drew attention to the verb of the scopic drive (*seeing*) as well as his emphasis on the *magical* power of change and his statement that a relationship, for him, needed to be *long-distance*. An intervention was made at the level of homophony of the signifier *distance*. It was put to him as *de-stance*. The intervention targeted his subjective position and the axis of the scopic drive at the level of his body.

As he elaborated his personal life, he likened his position in the world to that a *wizard* and a solitary inhabitant of a *moving castle*, who possessed the magical power to restore *youth and beauty* in women. The discovery (or reconstruction) of such a scenario, after the *de-stance* intervention in his narrative, changed the direction of the work towards questioning and exploring his original reasons for such positioning towards the Other. His attempt to avoid whatever he interpreted as excessive closeness to a loved one turned out to be fear of causing pain and suffering in his significant Other. This suggested a particular positioning in relation to the liveliness of the Other's desire. Being an all-powerful wizard with the magical power to restore and enhance someone else's life seemed to be his way of dealing with the Other's unknown desire. Wasn't this his strategy for nullifying the liveliness of the Other's desire? Moreover, wasn't his urge to turn back time (echoed in his motto of restoring youth in women) and his antipathy towards the passage of time, with all its unexpected twists and turns, manifested in his strategy of delay and procrastination?

As he questioned his desire, ideals, purpose and goals in life, he was convinced that he had become a *good wizard* who restored life and beauty to others. The *wizard* was a signifier obtained from the content of the fairy tale (fabric of the Real/mother tongue). His mother, who read him the fairy tale, also frequently complained of having sacrificed her *youth* and *beauty* for her children. He had constructed a symptom based on his mother's complaint and the fairy-tale wizard with restoring power. The *moving* seemed to be a precondition to fulfil his life mission – the precondition of being away from the maternal nest. The *good wizard* statement also contained an echo of the subject's ethical stance. Through the work of analysis, he gradually moved towards recognising this stance and began to question it, and this made it easier for him to face the Other's desire with much less guilt. His unconscious avoidance strategies became less rigid. His girlfriend informed him of her pregnancy and he was able to become a father, to anchor his moving castle. He said: "I am quite excited about what's coming!" He had learnt to dwell less on the past and the uncertainty of the future had become easier to face.

Psychosis and bedtime fairy tales

When they hear that a subject believes in magic, many clinicians might suspect psychosis. However, apart from the possibility of a cultural origin, such beliefs may be held by a neurotic subject, only in a position different from that of a psychotic. The possibility of magic might be a sort of guarantor (an Other), offering reassurance to the subject as he makes his way through life. Or the belief in magic may be a hope that acts as a substitute for the phallic jouissance by providing the neurotic subject with an appreciation of being alive – an aspiration to achieve success or overcome a difficult situation. For some subjects believing in magic can also signal a different modality of jouissance, outside and beyond the symptom, that is, the Other/feminine jouissance. In neurosis, elaboration of the theme of identification with a superhero/heroine, who possesses a magical power for change, targets a subjective position in relation to the *objet a* and the Other, rather than a libidinal, narcissistic investment on the ideal image of a superhero/heroine as is usually found in the clinic of psychosis.

In psychosis, there can be a solid certainty of being blessed eternally by a supernatural being or of possessing a supernatural power to put a curse on others. A psychotic subject's identification with a magical fairy or a heroic character can act as a point of gravity and hold down their mode of being in language. It can also create a life mission for them as a substitute for the symptom in neurosis. Such a subjective construction can help the psychotic subject to remain in a relationship with the Other and reduce the pain of being or the intrusion of the Real. The story a subject might tell himself, inspired by the characters in a fairy tale, can function at the level of ego formation and the subject's identity in his social bond. Such an Imaginary image of self supports a subject's knot of being. According to Lacan's reading of the case of James Joyce, the Irish writer, the sinthome (Joyce's style of writing) was equated with his ego (who he was as a writer). Such an equation between the ego and sinthome can also be interpreted as a perversion (Soler, 2018).

It is even possible to distinguish the sub-categories of psychosis based on the different functions that a fairy tale can operate for a psychotic subject. Believing in a supernatural or magical power might offer meaning to a melancholic subject, lessening the weight of a crippling guilt. In paranoia, the possessor of a superpower may be blamed for the subject's miseries in life. For a schizophrenic subject, belief in magic can operate at the dimension of meaning in language. According to Lacan, naming a bodily event (experiencing an excitation in the body or psyche) can act as a "quilting point", holding the signifier and signified together (Lacan, 1955–6). A psychotic subject's whole life can be organised around a meaning: having a magical power, so that they can fulfil a certain mission in the world. An identification with a character in fairy tales gives identity and meaning to their being, a meaning that helps them to punctuate a non-localised jouissance on their Real body. Such a mode of jouissance has to be worked through over and over again, each time that it overwhelms the subject.

To be an abandoned castle: two psychotic case studies

Case I

A patient might refer to the (possible) cause of his unsettling feelings or of events happening in his body as a magic spell that has been cast upon him. This might generate momentary relief from an intrusion of the Real. Moreover, such an act of naming can even enter into the lexicon of the patient as a libidinally charged term that occupies a central role in how he organises his life on a day-to-day basis. For one of my patients, *magic* was the name given to a type of momentary mental excitement that he felt from time to time. It was called "magic" by the patient, as he found that he was always full of new creative ideas for his work after experiencing this sensation (a sort of epiphany). His professional life was in the sphere of advertising: suggesting new ideas to promote various products. He remembered having experienced this excitement since late childhood. He recounted how, at the moment of turning of the TV one day as a child, he suddenly felt a *magical moment* in his head. He was compelled to jump up and down from intense excitement at the moment when the screen went completely dark. Later, he experienced a psychotic episode in young adulthood, followed by a depressive mood. During his depression, he developed a compulsive habit of turning the TV on and off, in the hope that the magical spark of excitement would recur. Later, in his twenties, after recovering from a long period of depression, he managed to find his way back to normality through artistic creation. All of his projects were, in fact, focused on effects obtained with lights and the theme of sudden on-off changes, similar to the magical moment of disappearance of light on the TV screen which he had experienced much earlier in life.

"Magic" in his terminology described the excitement coming from inside him, first felt intensely, then followed by a discharge: a sequence which was manifest in his creative work (outside his body). Creating artworks had functioned not only to organise an excessive jouissance on his body, but had also helped him to have a space and build relationships in his social life. In addition to the magical moment that he had experienced in childhood, his personal history included a few major instances of sudden, unexpected and radical change, similar to the magical moment of change in fairy tales. He had identified with a wizard character in a fairy tale of his childhood. He believed that he had an extraordinary ability to help people, like a white wizard. His mode of being in language changed over the course of the treatment. His relation to the passage of time had been constantly interrupted and this caused him enormous suffering, making it hard for him to keep up his daytime work pace. In the course of the treatment the concept of linear, as opposed to interrupted time began to have a meaning for him.

Case II

A young woman believed that she had a magical power and was able to live a second life, in parallel with her main life. This delusion had taken shape after she heard a supersonic noise coming from a military aircraft over her village during wartime. An aerial bombardment had begun and she ran for her life out of the village. Since then, the supersonic noise came back to her from time to time, just before convulsive and fainting attacks. The war had broken out when she was 3 years old, but her village had not been bombarded until she was a young teenager. She had grown up with a combination of war-related noises and fairy tales, and these two elements were patent in her narrative. Her terminology when she recounted her life story came mainly from folklore and fairy tales, as if her world was built inside another world, resonating with her delusional idea of having two parallel lives. Living with fairy tales was her way of dealing with the devastating circumstances of war. Such an approach to the anguish caused by war differed from the essence of a neurotic subject's desire or symptom, which might focus on what can be done to stop/avoid a war. For her, fairy tales involved a radical belief with abstract meaning, with which she was able to carry on living. The elements found in the tales had allowed her to symbolise the devastating events around her, as if the war was seen through the lens of a fairy tale. Based on the clear, black-and-white contrasts between *good* and *bad* wizards in fairy tales, she had found a system as a child with which she could make choices in her life. The *good wizard* was mainly associated with a metonymic chain of the aesthetic aspects of life, simplicity, naivety and weakness, while the *bad wizard* was responsible for whatever belonged to the underworld of secrecy and power. After she experienced the supersonic noise, she had become deeply unsettled, experiencing visions of running from a threat or seeing the dead bodies of her family members killed in the war. The theme of fairy tales in her narratives did help her to find a certain meaning, offering a sustainable structure for her psychical life. It was also her means of expressing the deep pain that she was suffering – that without which, however, she would be unable to live. Her eventual return to war zones, in order to help victims, alleviated some of her complaints of somatic pains with non-organic causes, transforming her perception of her own identity as someone who sought only revenge. Her mode of being and living was supported by her new sinthome as a nurse in warzones. After the war, she remained in a care home where she nursed the residents, who were war veterans.

Each subject can pick up a certain element from a fairy tale and work around it in their life. One patient had identified herself as a haunted, abandoned castle. She was appreciative of the pompous, grand narrative found in certain fairy tales. Her own perception of herself in the company of others was, as she said, that of an *extra-terrestrial*. She had formed an identity for herself by using a fairy-tale narrative. Her position in the language as an abandoned castle – something that would eventually be left behind and forgotten – made her social life difficult. Further details of her childhood revealed that such a position was, in fact, a defensive reaction to her caregiver's negligence and unkindness. Later in the work, she revisited this position and gradually became able to change her coping strategy towards the Other's demands and expectations. She preferred to remain a castle, still proud and grand, but no longer abandoned; a castle built far, far away from others, but which would nevertheless open her gates to the *mysterious explorer* from time to time, making allowance in a more patient and tolerant way for the presence of other people in her life. Fairy tales both supported her ego and appeared as a theme in some of her artworks. Her ego and her sinthome shared the same theme, but were not equated. The way in which she related to her artwork did not reflect her identity but was rather a way to "drag the pain out of her being".

In Chapter 4, we will pursue further the question of clinical diagnosis in psychoanalysis. How do we understand and differentiate the direction of the treatment in each clinical case based on the subject's mode of being in language? Is the detection of a certain psychical structure equivalent to pigeonholing analysands and patients in a specific clinical category, or, on the contrary, does it help us understand a subject's mode of dealing with the Other and jouissance?

To Ronak Khakban

Bibliography

Lacan, J. (1955–6). *The seminar of Jacques Lacan: Book III. The psychoses.* J.-A. Miller, ed., and R. Grigg (Trans.). London: Routledge, 1993.

Lacan, J. (1974–5). *Le séminaire livre XXII: R, S, I.* Paris: Seuil.

Lacan, J. (1975–6). *Le séminaire livre XXIII: Le sinthome.* Paris: Seuil.

Soler, C. (2018). *Lacan reading Joyce.* Devra Simiu (Trans.). London: Routledge.

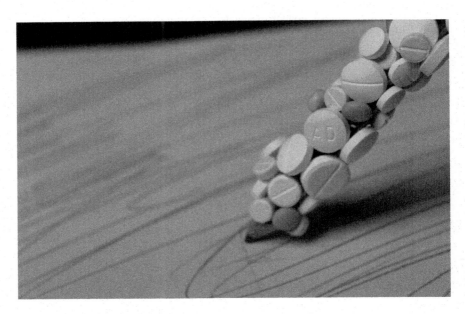

Figure 4.1 Amnesia, photograph by Bardia Moeini

Chapter 4

Psychoanalysis and clinical diagnosis

Introduction

Medieval ideas on the diagnosis of physical and mental un-wellness were derived from antiquity and Greek medicine, mainly from Galen and Hippocrates. Health depended on a balance between the four bodily elements (earth, air, fire and water) and four humours (blood, phlegm, yellow bile and black bile). Patients were considered to suffer from an illness if there was an imbalance between the aforementioned elements and humours. Diagnosis and the choice of treatment were also guided by Greek medicine, astrology and sorcery, the idea being that a condition was inflicted upon a suffering subject by the combined effects of bodily change and the universal elements. Avicenna, the Persian physician and thinker whose book, *The Canon*, was the medical textbook of reference until the eighteenth century, believed strongly in human intelligence and perceptual ability as key factors affecting health and illness. He was the first physician to suggest the idea of a syndrome. A condition – represented by a set of symptoms (symptomology) – was associated with an underlying issue. According to Avicenna, poor physical health could affect the soul. So his thoughts on human subjectivity (anticipating Descartes' *cogito*) were focused on human intelligence and perceptual ability.

The health or disease of the body had great importance for diagnosis of mental suffering in Avicenna's approach and throughout the Middle Ages, because it was supposed to be the determinant of "feelings" and feelings (before Freud's invention and Lacan's reinvention of the unconscious) were the touchstone of diagnosis, as well as the marker of well-being (prognosis) and the target and ultimate goal of a clinical treatment. Even today, such an approach orients many clinical approaches to a subject's mental health. The ideal was to find a balance between good and bad feelings. In the ancient approach, the life span of a human subject was divided into four stages: childhood (choleric), adolescence (sanguine), maturity (phlegmatic) and old age (melancholic). Each stage was marked by a specific quality, based on the dominance of a humour. This ancient approach to diagnosis is, however, at the opposite pole from modern psychiatry with its never-ending list of categories and sub-categories. The main difference seems to be between listening to the language of the body (the ancients) and listening to narratives around

DOI: 10.4324/9781003184799-5

bad feelings (the moderns). It is doubtful whether the modernisation of subjective suffering, with its urge to classification, offers a much better understanding of the cause and treatment of a condition than the more simple approach of the ancient world (the four humours model). Each may be useful to some suffering subjects, but neither says much about the actual cause of pain in our psychical life today. The pain and pleasure which are products of today's culture have an effect on our being. Physical illness or an imbalance of bodily elements (such as hormones) affect our sense of well-being, but, since Freud's invention of psychoanalysis – itself a product of culture – the main source of suffering lies between the complication of language and the incongruity of jouissance. Both Freud and Lacan used a much simpler way of categorising mental suffering, where unpleasant feelings – as undeniable and irrepressible elements – are considered to be the expression of a repressed thought or signifier.

In the ancient world, the sources of physical and mental discomfort were sought, not by listening to subjective narratives, but by examining the patient's blood, urine, stool and other bodily secretions. The skulls of patients were punctured to examine and cure mental disturbances long before the invention of lobectomy and electroconvulsive therapy! This might look like a precursor of today's laboratory testing, but it is not clear if medicine and magic were really separate. The intention of science was to make the unknown Real (that of science) known and distinct from an act of sorcery. The psychoanalytical act, however, aims at the alienating, anguish-provoking Real of our speaking being, which is not a product of intelligence. In psychoanalysis the Real has a subjective currency and cannot be discovered by the usual tools of medicine. Indeed it is not uncommon in contemporary culture to hear the psychoanalyst referred to as a witch or wizard! The Real of our being is not the same as the target of cognitive science, nor is it what is at issue in philosophical debates about perception (idealism versus realism). Psychoanalysis takes a third approach. It is both a product of the question about our being, and an ally/tool by which we can take the question on board.

In psychoanalysis, it would surely be an irony to conduct a treatment based on a diagnostic framework, since the psychoanalyst believes in the particularity of each subject's agency in choosing a position towards the Other of body and language, forming a desire and drive montage, and interpreting equivocation in order to make a signification that leads (or does not lead) to a symptom.

Lacan, following Freud's approach to diagnostic classification, spent three decades elaborating three main categories of psychical structure (neurosis, psychosis and perversion), arriving finally at his use of the Borromean knot as a model of the speaking being, particular to each subject of the unconscious.

Freud developed his theory of Oedipus complex while approaching the question of clinical diagnosis. The three psychical structures are the results or outcomes of the Oedipus complex. What was Lacan's take on Freudian Oedipal myth? Where did he position this theory in the clinic of psychoanalysis when he reread and criticised Freud's understanding of the subject's suffering? Let us review Lacan's reading from the Oedipal myth.

Oedipus, the true master

According to Lacan, Freud's best-known legacy, the Oedipus complex (named after the main protagonist of Sophocles' Theban plays), was Freud's own myth, created in order to deal with his grief over his father's death. The idea of the Oedipus complex can be found in Freud's work as early as his letters to Fliess in the 1890s. It then figures in *The Interpretation of Dreams* (1899), the *Dora* case (1901–5) and later in *Totem and Taboo* (1913–4) and his metapsychological article "The Unconscious (1915)". We will approach this fundamental Freudian theory through Lacan's reading in order to understand the difference between the different psychical structures that are a result or outcome of the Oedipus complex. Lacan pays attention to specific aspects of the tragedy of Oedipus in his critique of Freud's preoccupation with it. Lacan believed that Freud's myth needed to be analysed like any other symptom.

We will start by considering and analysing the myth from a Lacanian perspective. Lacan's reading of the Freudian myth starts from his 5th Seminar, and then is also prominent in 17th Seminar, where he introduces his four discourses as one possible substitute for the Oedipus complex. From 20th Seminar onwards, Lacan's approach to the clinic of the suffering subject focuses on the topological representation of the subject (the Lacanian Borromean knot) consisting of the three strings of R, S and I, which are mutually dependent and contain the object *a* in their intersection.

From 17th Seminar, and later in his Borromean knot, Lacan's theorisation of psychoanalysis becomes less and less phallocentric. In his teachings on the nature of subjectivity, we hear less and less about the phallus and more about a "knot of being". Lacan's suggestion is that "de-Oedipalisation" of clinical interpretation saves clinical work from stagnation and unnecessary resistance or perhaps from an abrupt termination, as happened in Freud's *Dora* case. Lacan starts from the Freudian diagnostic system and by elaborating the three planes of frustration, privation and castration of the phallus, he reintroduces the psychical structures of psychosis, neurosis, perversion and phobia. From the early 1950s onwards, the phallus is the signifier of lack in the first significant Other – lack as a sign of privation.

But how did Lacan de-phallicise the clinic of the subject? He did so in two steps:

1   By targeting the object of desire, which, for Freud, was the mother (her love/ attention/care). He takes up this object (the mother) and replaces it with a desire: a desire for knowledge. Then in 17th Seminar he asks what might be the nature of this knowledge that is sought. And he concludes that it is realisation of the impossibility of any knowledge, which can coincide with truth, since truth is always "half said" (mi-dire); (Lacan, 1969–70, p. 31)

2   He changes the currency of exchange with the Other from the phallus as a signifier of lack, where what is at stake is to be or to have the phallus

(discussed at length and in detail in 5th Seminar), to discourse. In 17th Seminar, he approaches the discourse of the hysteric and scrutinises the relationship between the hysteric and the master (who must always be a castrated master) in relation to the Freudian myth.

Lacan starts to analyse Freud's Oedipus complex and gently criticise it in 5th Seminar where, in the chapter entitled "The 3 moments of the Oedipus complex", he says that the first moment of the Oedipus complex occurs when the child takes the mother as a subject (not an object) of desire. So, the subject-to-be (the child) makes the Other his Other. This first Other (mOther) is a subject who is deprived of an object. In this context, Lacan introduces the function of the Real father and equates it with the Name of the Father. In his subsequent teaching, however, the Name of the Father changes to the plural form "Names" before giving way to the symptom, which is something that ultimately separates the child from the mOther. While the Real father comes across to the child as the castrating agent, who has the mOther's object of privation in his possession, the Symbolic father in Lacan's work can be anything at all except the mOther. Many children realise that the mother has a preoccupation in her life other than the child's own self. However, if this third agent (the Symbolic father) does not have a function operating on the mOther's desire, the best outcome of the Oedipus complex, namely neurosis, will not be achieved. The function of the Real father can be accepted and repressed, denied or disavowed or it can be cancelled out or foreclosed. It is up to the subject to submit or not submit to this function, to accept it and then cancel it or to disavow it. In terms of the logical time of the Oedipus complex, what comes first is not the relation to the phallus, but the function of the Real father. After taking up a position towards the function of the Real father/Name of the Father, the subject devises a strategy towards the phallus as a signifier of lack in the mOther. The subject wonders how to deal with this lack. There will be three possible outcomes – neurosis, psychosis or perversion – depending on which stance he adopts. Phobia in childhood acts as a revolving door, which can later develop into perversion, psychosis or neurosis. Phobia can be quite functional in helping the child to cope with anxiety when confronting primary jouissance.

In psychosis, the lack is not registered in the Other, meaning that the mOther does not come across as someone who is deprived of the Thing. In some cases, she can also be perceived as not castrated. Although the Symbolic father has been operative, the Name of the Father has been first realised but then cancelled out. Or, in some other cases of psychosis, we have an absence of both Symbolic and Real father. This could have happened due to the mother's failure to facilitate the child's introduction to the symbolic order and submission to the law of the castrating agent. Such circumstances can make a subject choose to remain bonded to the mother.

Who has castrated the mOther? Lacan asks in 5th Seminar. The Name of the Father is not the castrating agent for the mOther but for the child. Lacan adds here that this Name is a "depriver" of the mOther. It has deprived the mOther of an object without castrating her and holds the object of the mOther's privation/ desire. Lacan gives us a meaningful explanation for psychosis here: if the child recognises but does not accept the mother's privation, he might develop some sort of identification with the object of the mother's privation. This object, Lacan says, is a "rival" object to the child (Lacan, 1957–58, p. 169). This is one explanation, in the clinic of psychosis, for cases of copying or following religiously and rigidly in someone else's footsteps.

What happens in the second moment of the Oedipus complex after the child recognises the mOther as a subject? Referring once again to the case of Little Hans in 4th Seminar (devoted to the object relation) Lacan says that the second moment occurs when the child submits to the mOther's law – what he calls "being subjected to subjectification" (assujetissment in French). This moment is anxiety provoking. Such anxiety is a common feature in work with children and a phobia can be effective in mastering it. It is a response coming from the "subject-to-be". But difficulties arise when the phobic object becomes an all-purpose signifier, which is the case in Little Hans' phobia of the horse, which served as a substitute for all members of his family, indicating equality of rank between them all. So, there was no elevation of a specific figure in the family structure who could find the introduction to the Symbolic order – an introduction, which is much needed in order for a subject to reach an accessible form of enjoyment in life. The horse in Hans' world was his mother, his father, his sister and the phallus. The father in one of his dreams presented to Freud was downgraded to a plumber. Lacan says that Hans' phobia (fears) had, in fact, provided him with a zone beyond the sub-jectification anxiety.

Some Lacanian analysts read the *Little Hans* case as suggesting that the out-come of the Oedipus complex for Hans was a perverse structure. There are two main grounds for such a reading: the ego ideal for Hans was his sister rather than (as in hysteria) the idealised father; and his devotion in adult life to a career as opera director may suggest a narcissistic investment on the ego (equated with what Lacan calls the "sinthome").

Lacan approaches the *Little Hans* case through linguistics and tells us that the boy's mOther had provided the subject with a confusing message (ambiguity of the mother tongue) and that his father's words had not sufficed to cut through this ambiguous desire of the mOther. Because of this Hans was unable to inter-pret things differently and obtain a different outcome of his phobia in the second moment of the Oedipus complex. Although his phobia was eventually resolved, it was at a price. In other words, for Little Hans the mother underwent privation, but the father was not the depriver, that is, the person who held the object of her desire. In this context, Lacan gives us examples of perversion (fetishism and transvestism). In fetishism there is an imaginary identification with the mother and the child attaches himself to the object of the mother's privation/desire, while in transvestism, the child has identified with the imaginary phallus behind the mother's clothes.

This brings us to the third moment of the Oedipus complex, which can be called *the moment of truth*. Three things happen in this third moment: (1) being or having the object which satisfies the mother (when the child's demands come into play and meet a much-needed frustration on the part of the mother); (2) the father, who up until then had intervened in the Imaginary registers between subject and mother, is established as *the agent of law* whose law is different from that of the mother. Here, the father is the "supporter of the law" who can give the mother what she is deprived of. This law prohibits the subject (in his own interpretation) from being drowned in an excessive, morbid jouissance; (3) Freud tells us that at the end of the Oedipus complex, the subject identifies with the father, while Lacan believes that the subject identifies with the ego-ideal, which must go beyond the mOther in the Symbolic order so that the child can continue to appreciate being alive. This coincides with Lacan's account of phallic jouissance.

Later in his teaching, in 17th Seminar, Lacan appears disappointed by the way in which the Oedipal myth serves as a central theory of psychoanalysis and wonders about its suitability for understanding the divided subject. He raises once again the questions of the paternal metaphor, the object, lack and the phallus, very differently this time, and replace them all with knowledge, truth and discourse. The master is castrated. The object of desire, Lacan says, is a knowledge or, to be more precise, it is desire for what is impossible, namely the merging of truth with knowledge. Therefore, any myth or narrative can be a compromise built around the impossibility of knowing the truth and the whole truth. Which truth? The truth of the impossibility of enjoyment outside the law. Lacan developed this idea in 20th Seminar and thereafter. The questions we should ask in respect of 17th Seminar are: Who was Oedipus? Who/what is the master? What is castration? What role did knowledge play in Sophocles' tragedy? And what would be the price of knowing which eventually takes account of the outcome of the Oedipus complex?

Lacan notes that Freud's desire is both revealed and obscured in the myth of Oedipus and that it needs to be analysed like any other myth in analysis. We keep telling ourselves a particular myth or a story (it is dear to each one of us) in order to avoid the truth of the sexual non-rapport as well as our mortality. If, in Sophocles' tragedy, Oedipus finally becomes "complex free", it is not because he killed his father and slept with his mother, thereby fulfilling his desire. Oedipus blinds himself when he realises the truth of what he has done and that by serving justice he can save the city from the plague that has been sent as punishment for his acts. As Lacan says, he "castrates" (blinds) himself and that is why he is a true master, that is a castrated master: the master is always a castrated master in the development of the 4 discourses that Lacan carries out in 17th Seminar. Is it not the story that Oedipus repeats to himself after blinding himself, "I blinded", that is castrated, "myself to save the city from the plague", which enables him to resolve his complex? Unlike some interpreters who take Oedipus as someone who resolved his complex because he actually killed his father and slept with his mother, we see the resolution occurring in the action of his self-blinding. The impossibility of approaching the truth is well metaphorised in his blindness, and it is not only his self-blinding (to which Lacan draws our attention) but also the narrative that he produces around this action that counts as the result of the third moment of the Oedipus complex: "I saved the city by blinding myself".

What is more, according to the Freudian myth, Oedipus should have first desired his mother then killed her husband. But, as Lacan points out, Oedipus never knew his father and was unaware that the man, Laius, whom he killed, was his father. Lacan adds that Oedipus's desire was more focused on killing Laius than sleeping with Jocasta (Oedipus was also unaware that she was his mother). According to Lacan, Freud himself was a subject whose patricidal myth (the Oedipus complex) was, in fact, his defence against castration anxiety, corresponding to his guilt over the death of his own father, whom he idealised. The fact that the father is murdered in the Oedipus myth also shows us that the master is, in fact, immortal precisely because he has been murdered.

The next question we raised earlier was: what is castration? It is the impossibility imposed on unlimited enjoyment. To approach this question Lacan in 17th Seminar distinguishes the role of myth (Freud's Oedipal myth) or the Oedipus complex from castration anxiety. In 5th Seminar, the anxiety in the second moment of the Oedipus complex was linked to "being subjected to subjectification" (assujetissment). But in 17th Seminar, the anxiety is associated with confronting unlimited jouissance and how to come to term with the sexual non-rapport. What does this mean?

Lacan brings up the discourse of the hysteric by referring to the *Dora* case and approaches the castrated master and the Real father not as someone who is the holder of all the women in a clan, as in *Totem and Taboo* (this is, in fact, the opposite of being the Real father whose function counts in the Oedipus complex), but a father who *knows* all the answers. The castrated master knows all the answers but does not force his knowledge on the subject. This is a frequent experience in the clinic of hysteria when the analyst's interpretation is declined by the hysteric until the time arrives for him to sanction and allow the knowledge be held as meaningful. A knowledge which, of course, resides outside the Symbolic order.

In the myth, Oedipus first solves the sphinx's riddle (What walks on four legs in the morning, two at noon and three in the evening?). Interestingly, the answer is "man". His answer saves lives. He is rewarded by being made King of Thebes. In the second stage, when the city is ravaged by plague, he himself is the answer. This time, the answer is not rewarded by a kingdom but it acts as a moment of truth, proving that he is a good King: he had said that the person who committed the crime, which made the gods send the plague, must be punished. When he discovers the truth, that he himself is the criminal, he keeps his promise and blinds himself. As can be seen, the status of the knowledge produced is different in these two instances. In the first encounter, the knowledge produced is a fact, "the man", and is rewarded. In the second, the answer is "Oedipus" and comes with a consequence that he has to bear painfully. He is the cause of people's suffering. As a true master, recognising the price that comes with knowing the truth, he castrates himself and frees his people from the plague. The motif of "saving my people" as a subjective narrative is the knowledge produced after confronting the truth. The knowledge originates from the realm of the subject and enables Oedipus to carry on living with the impossible truth which is always, according to Lacan, only half-said. It is half-said because the other half (that would make it whole) is always dangerous and loaded with morbid jouissance. The Real father (a true, castrated master) in this myth is Oedipus himself who forbids the excessive, unlimited jouissance by his act of blinding himself. In this myth, he is the agent who executes the law on himself.

Was Oedipus' act similar to the function of fear of horses for Little Hans? In Hans' case, the horse phobia is an all-purpose signifier. While this signifier reduces his castration anxiety in the second moment of the Oedipus complex, it does not carry the object of his mother's privation. In other words, his phobia does not act like a Real father. He himself remains in the position of the object of his mother's desire caring for his younger sister as his ego ideal. His biological father is outside the arrangement he has formed with the object a. By contrast, Oedipus' act can be seen as the third moment of the Oedipus complex: after being confronted with the impossibility of unlimited jouissance and after enduring castration anxiety, he pays the price and castrates himself. The Oracle gives him the opportunity to save the city and he willingly submits to the law of prohibition.

Unlike Oedipus who became the castrated master, in Freud's *Dora* case, the subject, Dora, starts seeking a master. Her father is impotent and in her dream he is dead. This is where Lacan starts his re-reading of the case in 17th Seminar. It is only death which is beyond death, meaning there is nothing beyond an absolute termination. Lacan says that for Dora, unlike Little Hans, the father seemed to be perceived as "immortal". Dora's father still had the power of seduction for Frau K. despite being impotent in reality. He is idealised. So, in Dora's eyes he was able to answer the impossible question of sexuality in a woman (Frau K.) Again, Dora seems to be more interested in the knowledge than in sexual intercourse: she wants knowledge regarding the fundamental question of hysteria, "What does a woman want?" This is where Lacan reads a neurotic subject's desire as a desire to know. But does she really want to know the answer in order to be fulfilled and free from her doubts? The answer is No! This was, in fact, Freud's failure in Dora's case. Freud thought of himself as a master in Dora's world and assumed that by offering her knowledge related to her sexuality, he would cure her.

Lacan says of hysteria that the hysteric "unmasks" the master's function "with which she remains united" while refusing to be the object of the Other's desire (Lacan, 1969–70, p. 94). What does this mean? She makes the Other work and produce knowledge. As such she allows the master to play all his cards. She takes pleasure in knowing all the cards in the master's hand. Now he is unmasked and safe to approach. According to Lacan's reading of the dynamic between Frau K. and Dora, Dora identifies with Frau K. because Frau K. knows how to sustain the desire of Dora's idealised father. She identifies with "the master's jouissance", as

Lacan says (Lacan, 1969–70, p. 96). In her case, the father is dead, which means not only that he is idealised, but also that the dead father has prohibited the subject from unlimited jouissance. Her father is the Real father and the Real father is dead, that is immortal and idealised. The Real father "guards jouissance" (Lacan, 1969–70, p. 123). In the hysteric's discourse, the master is someone who has all the knowledge, but not so much that the hysteric subject will agree to give herself in exchange for his knowledge. Lacan says, "she reigns, and he does not govern" (Lacan, 1969–70, p. 129). A hysteric wants to be left space, room, a lack to play with, in order to have her own input and manoeuvre. That is why the hysteric is said to embody the truth of the master.

We might ask why Lacan uses the discourse of the hysteric to approach once again the question of castration after rejecting the Freudian Oedipus complex? Lacan connects the hysteric's discourse with that of the master. The hysteric's relation to the master and the Other, truth and knowledge, teaches us that the subject is not divided simply as a result of a given truth/fact; rather the divided subject has agency and puts the master to work so that he produces knowledge, with which the subject can *approach the truth*. In analysis, an analysand seeks a knowledge which concerns the sexual non-rapport and his/her sexuality in order to come closer to the anxiety-provoking, impossible truth. Right until the last moment the analysand seeks an exchange whereby he could trade the produced knowledge or merge it with the truth of the sexual non-rapport and his mortality. And finally, let us not forget that, in the clinic of psychoanalysis, every analysand's discourse is a hysteric's discourse at the beginning of the treatment before approaching and eventually changing into the analytic discourse.

In the next part, we will approach the question of differential diagnosis by elaborating the fundamental differences between two psychical structures (neurosis and psychosis) in relation to language and jouissance. Then, we will see why making a diagnosis matters in the clinic of psychoanalysis, although the narratives around the demand for a cure are often the same across different structures. The question then is: why does orienting of the clinical framework matter at all and at what level does a diagnosis affect the direction of the treatment?

Psychoanalysis and psychical structures

"I'm not sure how to describe my feelings. I feel at unease and worried. It becomes intense from a moment to another during a day. It haunts my body. It's like living in fear. I feel myself again, when it has gone. Life has lost its savour and I don't have the energy to do my daily chores and meet my commitments or even to care about myself and others".

In years of clinical practice, this is a narrative I have heard at the first consultation from many patients when they describe their emotional state. How can the work of analysis be oriented in each individual case, when the initial complaints resemble each other and the demand for a cure has one common motif, to feel better?

In psychoanalysis, it is well known that naming the condition is not the same as making a diagnosis. The condition signifies that a subject is cornered by his or her suffering, which they cannot understand but which they certainly feel. If the patient has come as far as the analyst's consulting room, their suffering is probably serious and persistent, distinct from transient, everyday dissatisfaction, nervousness, anger, stress, embarrassment, guilt or disappointment. The unpleasant feeling, which has incited the subject to seek help or given them a strong desire to know its root (the repressed idea), can appear in psychosis as well as in neurosis or perversion.

In neurosis, for example, a sense of guilt can be the result of acting on an unconscious desire (Lacan, 1959–60) or a sense of unbearable anxiety can indicate that a symptom has failed to translate a mode of jouissance in the unconscious for the neurotic subject, leaving them exposed to the pain of being in the Real. The ultimate transformation of all unpleasant feelings generates a painful state, which Lacan called "anguish" (angoisse) (Lacan, 1962–63). It is a state that can leave the subject insecure in the world (in language). An earlier lack of being (before forming a desire) is re-experienced without the support or mediation of a fantasy. Lacanian *manque-a-être* or *wanting to be* (Lacan, 1966d) indicates a necessary lack for a subject to form a desire. To be or to have what is lacking in the first significant Other constitutes the desire with which a subject's being becomes meaningful and less painful. In other words, long after alienation and separation from the Other (Lacan, 1963–64), the neurotic subject has once again felt the marks of primary jouissance which is the fabric of Real. An example from cinema might help to illustrate this. When Neo, the hero of the film, *The Matrix*, realises the truth of what he and everyone else had taken to be reality – that it is, in fact, a machine-generated phantasmagoria projected into the brains of human bodies stacked in a huge incubator – and decides to rebel and join the Morpheus resistance group, he is alienated and separated from the machine (the Matrix), but he bears on his body the marks of his previous incubation inside it as scars down his back, where he has been "unplugged". This is a fine metaphor for the marks of jouissance we carry through life after finding our way out of an opaque, primary jouissance (the mother tongue) (Lacan, 1975–76). These marks are a subjective reminder of the jouissance from which, much earlier in life, the subject once managed to escape through signification. But, in later life, an encounter with a situation – a repetition of the same pattern between subject and the Other – might corner the subject once again, and the invisible marks of primary jouissance generate anxiety and fear (anguish) for the subject. If the neurotic subject comes to analysis, the structure of the symptom will ultimately be altered or modified by working through the subjective signification, a process that offers a new purpose or meaning for his mode of being. An autonomy in the knot of being enables the subject to sustain in language and have access to *phallic* jouissance, which is an accessible form of jouissance.

Taking Neo in *The Matrix* as a case of neurosis, we see how his agency as a subject comes into question in the scene where he must choose between two pills, one of which will keep him inside the Matrix illusion, while the other will propel him into naked reality. Of course, decisions in real life are far more complicated and the situations (if any), in which a subject makes such a profound choice, require a questioning of drive arrangements, unconscious desire and the function of the symptom at a definite moment, in order to make an act that comes from the unconscious. Nevertheless, Neo's choice of the red (the "reality") pill can be taken as illustrative of the moment when a subject submits to the phallic significa-tion. If such submission takes place, the subject can appreciate the fact of being alive and embark upon a journey to fulfil his or her purpose in life. This journey is the scenario of a neurotic subject's unconscious desire. The desire is an envelope for much deeper and disturbing unconscious wishes (involving sex and violence), which can manifest themselves in disguise and change during a subject's life span, or can be passed on to the next generation, as both Lacan and Freud believed. Subjects who have recognised the function of the Name of the Father(s), as a proper name with the specific function of castration, and have managed to fash-ion a symptom based on their understanding of the equivocal narratives of their care giver in early childhood, tend to base their destiny in life upon their subjec-tive construction as their new narrative. Such narratives vary from one subject to another, generating a particular mode of jouissance for their being. The narrative may, for instance, be a lifelong story about the repaying of a debt or compensa-tion for an act committed by the previous generation, an act which is subjectively interpreted as misconduct or as a shortcoming. Or, similar to the story of *The Lion King*, if the subject's birth is celebrated as a gift to the universe, he or she (if they recognise and accept lack as castration in the Other) might be moved to either present themself as a gift to humanity later in life or to invent a missing piece of the puzzle of creation in order to rescue human beings. In neurosis, all versions of such stories are unconscious and the truth of their essence in personal narratives is uncertain. Expressed in the terms of Lacan's early works on signification and subject formation, neurosis would involve a solid bar between the signifier and signified (Lacan, 1966c). So the neurotic subject gives meaning to his being in language and, based on the signification of the phallus, an unconscious scenario (fantasy) supports the symptom and hence the knot of their being. Although Lacan in his earlier works referred to the symptom as metaphor and desire as metonymy, his later work on the Borromean knot – as a topological representation of the sub-ject – considers the symptom as something that ultimately separates the subject from primary jouissance (the mother tongue) (Lacan, 1975–76).

In contrast with the neurotic use of language, in psychosis painful conse-quences follow from the breakdown of a "makeshift" arrangement, created by the subject, between the Imaginary and Real registers. An armour – a means of defence against the Real – is somehow cancelled. In neurosis the bar between signifier and signified is solid, and the signification has led to symptom forma-tion, but in psychosis meaning can constantly change or be crystallised around a single motto. In his reading of the *Wolfman* case history, Lacan tendentiously used the term "foreclosure" (French "forclusion") to translate Freud's "Verwerfung" (literally "throwing away") (Lacan, 1966b). The psychotic subject, who, according to Lacan, has first recognised the third party (the Name of the Father) and then *foreclosed* the contract with that party for various reasons, is consumed by language (Lacan, 1955–56). The place of the subject, therefore, is constantly changing. A loss was recognised in the Other earlier in the subject's life but was negated and returns to the subject from the Real in the form of psychotic phenomena: delusional thoughts and hallucinations (an "Aufhebung", where something is used in a new form). For instance, in the case of Judge Schreber, Lacan identifies the patient's "push to the woman" (pousse à la femme) – the fantasy of being God's wife – as his particular psychotic solution (Lacan, 1972). Schreber's non-negativised jouissance was localised in the belief that he was the wife of God. Here we see a marked contrast, in work with psychotic subjects, between psychoanalysts and psychiatrists. For the psychiatrist, delusions and hallucinations justify pessimism about the outcome of the treatment. By contrast, the psychoanalyst believes that a psychotic subject can make use of the return of the Real, which is manifested in such delusions and hallucinations, in a way that helps him or her to sustain their mode of being.

As early as his Rome Discourse of 1953 (Lacan, 1966a) and the third year of his Seminar, Lacan refers to the psychotic subject's relation to language as that of a subject who is spoken by language. At this point of his teaching, the Name of the Father, which as a concept in Lacan's work, ultimately transforms into the knot that ties together the R, S and I triad through the symptom, is the "point de capiton" (quilting point or anchorage) between signifier and signified (Lacan, 1955–6). Its foreclosure has consequences for the subject's sexuation as well as his/her life in society. When the subject's being is not anchored, the knot of the subject's being – between language and jouissance – is in danger of being unravelled. According to Freud's approach in his 1915 article "The Unconscious", the difference between psychosis and neurosis is that, in psychosis, the link between word presentation and thing presentation is severed, while in neurosis the thing presentation is repressed (Freud, 1915). Lacan's understanding of Freud makes the thing presentation a missing signifier and has the Name of the Father as a further signifier, which, in some way, stands for the gap left by that missing signifier. The neurotic symptom is formed to give meaning to the subject's mode of being. In psychosis, refusal to submit to the phallic signification makes the subject unable to access some of the symbolic dimensions of language; therefore, the domain of language is limited to certain types of word connections, as manifested in the psychotic subject's symptomology at the level of speech. "Méconnaissance", the term which Lacan used in early 1950s referring to psychotic phenomena, is not a false recognition of the self; rather it is negating what is recognised: the signifier of the Name of the Father, a signifier unlike any other signifiers in discourse. Like a proper name, it does not change its meaning in any given context and is defined by its function – that of facilitating the phallic signification. This name is not necessarily the same as a symbolic agent operating as a separator between the child and the care giver. In the Freudian Oedipal myth, it is the one who is exempt from castration. In the process of phallic signification, the Name of the Father is a cornerstone which is employed by the subject to interpret the equivocal narratives of the mother tongue.

Why does a subject need phallic signification? Is phallic signification the only possible way to be sustained as a sexed and social being? It might be asked why a subject should submit to the law of the father and form a phallic signification, and in some cases of autism and psychosis, where the real father is himself an embodiment of the law, this refusal has indeed occurred (the subject recognises, but refuses to submit to this law). But the function of the paternal metaphor is only to establish a prohibition that limits excessive jouissance, giving a structure to maternal law. It can be the light at the end of the tunnel for a subject who is at a loss to come to terms with constant ambiguity in the dark, opaque equivocation of the mother tongue (as we discussed in the previous chapter, Lacan referred to alienation and separation in the process of subject formation as involving inevitable loss, similar to the highwayman's "Your money or your life!") (Lacan, 1963–64). The phallic signification gives a subject access to limited and accessible form of jouissance which is the phallic jouissance. Through the acceptance of castration, the jouissance will be organised around certain areas in the body (the erogenous zones) and the body will be perceived as a whole. Otherwise – as happens in some cases of psychosis – the function of the body takes on a whole different meaning. The body can be the target of an attack from excessive jouissance, leading to self-harm or the urge to carry out a series of medical/cosmetic interventions on the body. Such interventions can be understood as an attempt to obstruct the return of the Real to the body and psyche. By contrast, hypochondriasis in conversion hysteria can be a dysfunctional symptom, which indexed the Real but translated a troubling form of jouissance for the subject. In one clinical case, a neurotic subject, towards the end of the analytical work, eventually found a way to understand her torturing hypochondriasis. She interpreted her numerous complaints about her physical illnesses – mainly focused around her respiratory system – as her understanding of a narrative about her birth, which she had heard repeated since her early childhood. She was the last child to her parents, with a significant age gap to her siblings. Her mother had jokingly said that my patient was so "stubborn" (meaning that she had such a strong desire to live) that she was born healthy despite several attempts to abort the pregnancy. In a final threat to her arrival in this world, she was born with the umbilical cord around her neck and in adult life she carried the mother's death wish against her (from before her birth) as an illness of her respiratory system, which seemed to be of a hysterical nature. In her adult life, she had survived a number of life-threatening accidents. Despite a strong desire to survive (to survive rather than live), her mode of being was in pain and she complained of the agony of anxiety. Later in the work she interpreted her hypochondriasis as a way of being cared for, loved and wanted. Based on her unconscious understanding of her mother's attempts on her life in the womb, she had formed a symptom to make sense of her life. Although she intensely disliked medical practitioners (they made her anxious), she was in their care most of the time and had many doctor friends. She had come to me because I was a medical doctor as well as a psychoanalyst. Working through this paradoxical relation to the signifier of *health care* (in her narratives), a new path became available to this analysand for elaborating her own unconscious interpretation and symptom formation.

Psychical structures and the clinic

Lacan's work in theorising psychosis and psychotic phenomenon has made the question of diagnosis highly relevant to the clinic of psychoanalysis. Differentiating between psychosis and neurosis is helpful in order to avoid stagnation, repetition (as the resistance of the unconscious), acting-out or the patient's premature abandonment of the work. However, in some cases such differentiation does not happen very early in the work, or it might not be an urgent necessity.

In a 2016 scene from the last season of an HBO TV series, *Person of Interest*, the memories of an artificial intelligent, called simply "The Machine" (gendered as female in the series), are restored by its creator, Harold Finch. The Machine was built to predict terrorist acts by accessing all electronic surveillance and communication devices worldwide. However, after a series of events, her existence and function were threatened by a rival machine, called "Samaritan", operating under government control. The Machine was intentionally shut down (to save her from attack), but now needs to get back online to pursue her benevolent cause.

When Finch resuscitates the Machine, she seems to have lost her ability to process data and keeps making mistakes in predicting outcomes. The Machine has gone mad! Over-exposure to the bitter Real of the world has led her to devise a simple way of categorising people as good and bad and deciding their fates accordingly.

When Finch runs a diagnostic test, he realises that the Machine's psychical time has changed to Day R. In mathematics, R stands for the real numbers and Day R in this context means "every day" since the inception/birth of the Machine, which is reliving over and over a painful moment in the past with no mediation or limit. That painful moment occurred at the Machine's birth, when, in order to make her fit for her creator's purpose/desire, she was killed/shut down 42 times (each time that she began to show an ability to deceive, distort language or, perhaps, manifest her own desire). For the Machine, being in Day-R mode meant constantly re-experiencing her creator's death wish against her as a desiring subject. This was generating a great deal of suffering and affecting the Machine's capacity to function properly, even to the extent of hiring an assassin to inflict an act of terror on Finch's friend, Reese, who had saved lives with the help of the Machine many times in the past. Finch addresses the problem by installing an anchor in the Machine's core: a time metric. Finch acknowledges the Machine's feelings and confesses his own mistakes. He shows his own lack – his naivety and simple, narrow-minded understanding of good and evil – and reminds the Machine that he and the times have now changed.

Was the Machine's suffering a case of triggered psychosis or was she an unsettled neurotic who was re-experiencing the marks of overwhelming primary jouissance (primary trauma) at that particular moment in adult life?

The Machine was in crisis, like many patients we see in the clinic, whose pain is usually articulated as an extreme form of anxiety, fear and insecurity. How do we listen to their narratives? What should we look for in order to help them anchor their being in the present? What is a psychoanalytical response to the moment of crisis without the compass of a structural diagnosis?

The Machine's condition could be a case of psychosis, and her being is sustained by Finch's intervention on time metrics, which allows her to re-evaluate her history. He acknowledged her feelings, his own flaws and provided help in accordance with her own logic. This is an approach we might use in the clinic of some psychotic patients. Each subject wants to form and sustain their mode of being – between language and jouissance – in a certain, subjective way. What some psychotics seek in the work is to organise their thoughts by constructing their history, so that they can organise their sex and social lives "here and now". Other psychotics need lifelong support from clinical work as a point of reference or substitute for the gaze of a caregiver. Or there are patients who strive to form a sinthome, by which R.S.I can hold together. The limit and logic of access to language and jouissance will be different in each case. When we believe we are dealing with psychosis, we need to think how we can support the knotting of the three registers. In the absence of a compromise formation (the symptom), a psychotic patient needs a purpose in life in order to continue having tolerable access to the jouissance of their being. A compromise that can stop constant slippage of the bar between the S and s is needed to protect the subject from a living hell, like that of the Machine, which experienced the anguish of the death drive over and over.

On the other hand, the Machine could be a neurotic patient in crisis (it is not uncommon to receive highly anxious neurotics), where the Real of maternal jouissance – reliving a painful past – was expressed through the affect of anguish in an acting-out (hiring and paying an assassin to kill Reese). Finch's intervention can then be understood as therapeutic (acknowledging her feelings), but also as pushing the Machine towards the Real of her underlying desire: being an assistant to decent humans and not to an assassin.

Also in this vignette the Machine (as neurotic subject) is caught between the jouissance of her creator, Finch (the Jouissance of God) and her own desire to kill those she supposes to be evil-doers. She has instructed a hit-woman to kill Finch's friend, an ex-military man who had been an assassin, but has recently reformed. The Machine's logic is that a killer is a killer, and as she was designed to save lives (her symptom) he is a natural target. Torn between her unconscious desire as the path of metonymy, which was formed to protect her being against the Real of jouissance, and the Jouissance of God, she acted upon her own ethical stance: hiring an assassin to kill the guilty man. Following the intervention by Finch, who seemed to her to be a non-castrated God (similar to the transference love onto the subject-supposed-to-know at the beginning of a treatment of hysteria), she was eventually able to calm down and listen. In the next few days, her new symptom resumed its function by giving her being a new purpose: helping Finch and his crew to find the actual source of violence.

What the vignette shows is that, regardless of the subject's psychical structure, the analyst's intervention took the right course by alleviating the subjective crisis without obstructing the possibility of further exploration of unconscious knowledge (in case of neurosis) or without risking an episode of madness (in case of psychosis). Sometimes, in other words, the clinician's patience and acknowledgment of the pain would be the first step to prevent irreversible consequences in the clinic, even without a clear diagnosis. However, there are some cases when diagnosis is an urgent necessity soon after the beginning of the treatment. After making a diagnosis, the direction of the treatment would be based on the path, which the subject wants to pursue. Not all neurotics are prepared for potentially disturbing discoveries any time soon or ever.

A few years ago, I received a request for psychoanalytical treatment from a female patient. She was adamant about the type of therapy she wanted (psychoanalysis) and was keen to start work promptly. Her main complaint concerned her love life. She had just started a new relationship and was concerned about losing her lover due to her *old habits*. She said that her usual approach to relationships had always been to take the *carer and provider* role in relation to her partner. This had made her *exhausted* and she did not want to repeat the mistakes of her past in her new relationship, in which she felt appreciated. Exploring her narratives around an *old mistake* revealed a fear of *burning out* and yet not being appreciated. "My last partner used to avoid me all the time and it was noticed by my friends and family", she said. When I was curious to know why the significant other had "avoided her", she was puzzled too and wanted to know why. She was a mother of three children with a steady professional life, excited to be starting a new romance after ending a long-term relationship. A brief look at her history in our first meeting indicated a problematic relationship with her mother since childhood. She had helped her mother to separate from her abusive father. She was critical of her brother, who still lived with their mother, and she had a loving relationship with her elder sister. She had left her home country and resided in various countries before coming to London. It seemed that "moving away" from the Other had historically served her well in terms of giving her autonomy. However, I was unsure whether such a compromise was the symptom of a neurosis, or a temporary solution to tie together the knots of being in a psychotic subject. There had been no symptomology that suggested madness in all her 55 years of life and her uncertainty and confusion regarding the reasons behind some of her actions seemed to be more in accordance with a neurotic *passage à l'acte* in the Lacanian sense (Lacan, 1962–63). However, the precision with which she formulated what she wanted, based on a description of her childhood, flagged up an underlying psychotic structure. At first, I thought that I would be able to take my time making a diagnosis in her case by listening to her narratives in upcoming sessions, as she seemed committed to pursuing the treatment. However, she demanded an online arrangement for the work and the reality of her circumstances (working abroad most of the year) did indeed make it hard to have sessions in person. I needed a diagnostic orientation in order to handle her demand – to accept or to frustrate it in order to push her towards the Real of her desire. The question of diagnosis seemed urgent, and I was still in doubt. I did not have much time to search for a symptom, unconscious desire or any other resonances that would indicate submission or refusal to submit to the phallic signification (justifying a diagnosis of neurosis or of psychosis).

Although, on the surface, the material seemed to indicate a neurotic structure, her mode of speech was not symptomatic and there were elements in her case that made me inclined towards a psychotic structure: the exclusion of the Other in her discourse and her certainty as to what made her ill. In all her narratives – from her relationship with her *manipulative* mother to an *avoidant* long-term partner – the priority of her own wellbeing (a narcissistic position), directly affected by the Other's wrong-doing. and the certainty she attached to such a dyadic relation was striking. She mentioned that she had never felt *appreciated enough* for the sacrifices she had made for other people. She believed that she had reached a point where *enough was enough* and wanted to change the pattern as quickly as possible. Hearing her description of a *manipulative* mother, with whom she had felt *unsafe* and noting her keenness to keep a safe distance from the Other in her demand for online sessions, it seemed to me that the need to "feel safe" was a definitive factor. After only one meeting, it seemed to me that a correct diagnosis would be decisive for whether she continued the work or cut it short or perhaps pursued an acting-out. I decided to go with psychosis, which ultimately turned out to be the correct diagnosis. I agreed to online sessions and after a short while she decided to move to a male analyst in order to be even further away from a jouissance which had remained unindexed for her much earlier in life.

Conclusion

In this chapter I have tried to approach the question of needing a diagnosis and how we listen to a subject's narrative when he is suffering. What can possibly give us an idea about the subject's structural positioning towards the Other's and his own lack of being? The question of diagnosis can decide for the psychoanalytical act. How to listen, in itself, can be an analytical act in psychoanalysis. Overcoming the habit of maintaining a firm belief in knowledge is a long process for each psychoanalyst to work through. Such a belief might prevent an analyst to listen to the analysand's unconscious narrative and dynamic. In other words, "what should I search for in a session?" can be a real pitfall preventing the analyst from having fresh ears to listen with. Making a diagnosis is, in fact, learning how to listen to the unconscious.

Making a diagnosis can be difficult and yet crucial for an answer to the question of how to handle the subject's demand. Time (the analyst's patience) and the way he listens are the analyst's allies for proper diagnosis, and this is the reason why the preliminary sessions can sometimes be quite long. In some cases, diagnosis can only be made retrospectively and there are cases where a diagnosis is only obtained when the treatment is terminated.

In psychoanalysis the magic happens when a subject becomes tuned with their knot of being. Regardless of structural diagnosis, what matters is to prevent the subjective knot from unravelling. The knot of our being can be supported by a symptom/sinthome (the latter as the product of psychoanalysis), or by finding a way to knot the R.S.I. rings together without the mediation of a symptom, perhaps by finding a purpose in life. In psychosis it may be possible in adult life to compensate for the lack of phallic signification, if the subject wants and is able to do so. But such compensation is out of question in some cases of psychosis. Likewise in neurosis, a will to change, unmake and remake, or construct anew a compromise to index an overwhelming state of jouissance depends on the subject's agency and the ethics he forms for himself. States of feeling and emotion (language without discourse), pain and suffering, lightness or heaviness of being can be expressed in the same manner in the clinic across different psychical structures. Ultimately, it is the manner of a subject's agency in forming a defence against unpleasant states that distinguishes one case from another.

Bibliography

Freud, S. (1899). The interpretation of dreams. In: J. Strachey, ed., *The standard edition of the complete psychological works of Sigmund Freud, vol. 4.* London: Vintage, 2001.

Freud, S. (1901–5). Fragment of an analysis of a case of hysteria. In: J. Strachey, ed., *The standard edition of the complete psychological works of Sigmund Freud, vol. 7.* London: Vintage, 2001, pp. 3–122.

Freud, S. (1913–4). Totem and taboo. In: J. Strachey, ed. *The standard edition of the complete psychological works of Sigmund Freud, vol. 13.* London: Vintage, 2001, pp. 1–162.

Freud, S. (1915). The unconscious. In: J. Strachey, ed., *The standard edition of the complete psychological works of Sigmund Freud, vol. XIv.* London: Vintage, 2001, pp. 159–215.

Lacan, J. (1955–6). *The seminar of Jacques Lacan: Book III: The psychoses.* Jacques-Alain Miller (Ed.) and Russell Grigg (Trans.). London: Routledge, 1993.

Lacan, J. (1957–8). *The seminar of Jacque Lacan: BookV: Formations of the Unconscious.* Russell Grigg (Trans.). Cambridge: Polity Press, 2017.

Lacan, J. (1959–60). *The seminar of Jacque Lacan: Book VII: The ethics of psychoanalysis.* Dennis Porter (Trans.). London: Routledge.

Lacan, J. (1962–3). *The seminar of Jacque Lacan: Book X: Anxiety.* A. R. Price (Trans.). Cambridge: Polity Press.

Lacan, J. (1963–4). *The seminar of Jacque Lacan: Book XI: Four fundamental concepts of psychoanalysis.* Alan Sheridan (Trans.). New York and London: Norton.

Lacan, J. (1966a). *Écrits: The function and field of speech and language, 1953.* Bruce Fink (Trans.). New York and London: Norton, pp. 237–268.

Lacan, J. (1966b). *Écrits: Introduction to Jean Hyppolite's commentrry on Freud's "Verneinung", 1954.* Bruce Fink (Trans.). New York and London: Norton, pp. 308–333.

Lacan, J. (1966c). *Écrits: The Instance of the letter in the Unconscious, or reason since Freud, 1957.* Bruce Fink (Trans.). New York and London: Norton, pp. 412–455.

Lacan, J. (1966d). *Écrits: The direction of the treatment and the principles of its power, 1958*. Bruce Fink (Trans.). New York and London: Norton, pp. 489–542.

Lacan, J. (1969–70). *The seminar of Jacque Lacan: Book XVII: The other side of psychoanalysis*. Russell Grigg (Trans.). London: Norton.

Lacan, J. (1973). *Scilicet 4: L"étourdit, 1972*. Paris: Seuil, pp. 5–52.

Lacan, J. (1975–6). *Le séminaire livre XXIII: Le sinthome*. Paris: Seuil.

Figure 5.1 The Phantom, photograph by Bardia Moeini

Chapter 5

The body

Phantom of horror

Horror films vary in their plots and situations, but they all share certain devices that lead to the unexpected violence inflicted upon the protagonists. This is the chief motif of the horror genre. What makes the plot is how the characters tackle their destiny – regardless of what sort of ending, happy or violent, awaits them. But, unlike fairy tales, where a hero/heroine fights against evil to break a spell and which finally endorse a "happy ever after" ending, horror stories cannot allow a return to order, to the same as was before the encounter with the uncanny. The super-natural creature carries on living, to haunt, intimidate and destroy its future victims. In a horror narrative, one can expect a victim to die or change dramatically after seeing what is behind the mask; or he is kept alive or awake to experience torture. Despite the disaster that will ensue after the appearance of the horrible, there is typically a temptation on the part of the victim to see, unravel and discover what lies beneath the façade. Otherwise, what would the film be about?

Temptation is often said to be from the devil. The dominant theme in all religious doctrines (not least that of the health advisor and the medical profession) is how to resist, fight against or avoid a situation that provokes temptation, which many find irresistible at the moment of encounter and which is, in large part, an urge, not to enjoy what is offered but to know more about it. Although the attempt to gain such knowledge may come with a price, the subject of the unconscious might nevertheless choose to risk the consequences.

What can a *temptation* be from a psychoanalytical perspective for the subject of the unconscious? A temptation is something that cannot simply be ignored. What tempts or provokes each subject and how does he choose to respond and deal with the cause of such a temptation? These questions concern a choice; a choice to be made by each subject, based on his ethical stance in the language as a sexed being. This question of how to respond, face and maybe go through such an experience of uncanny excitation is what psychoanalysis is interested in.

The experience of encountering what lies behind the curtain can sometimes send a subject to a state of living hell. In a scene from the 2016 movie, *Doctor Strange*, after supervillain Kaecilius has been finally defeated in his battle

DOI: 10.4324/9781003184799-6

with Strange, he has to bear living hell for all eternity when he is sent to the *dark dimension*. His aim had always been to grasp absolute power. The wish was finally granted, but at a huge price. To unmask the truth at the heart of this super-natural power meant to be consumed by its flames. Temptation may, at first, be only a tickle before it is magnified into a stronger lust and the subject is consumed by the blaze of what lies behind the curtain. Kaecilius was not merely in search of a truth or knowledge to support his position in the language – he sought to become the horror behind the barrier. Ultimately, he was able to see the unlimited, infinite power, and it involved the disintegration of every inch of his body. In that dimen-sion (the inferno of darkness), the dark power inhibited him, instead of offering access to knowledge (the knowledge of a truth) that could give access to tolerable excitation.

Lacan, in his seminar on anxiety, likens the anxiety felt by a subject in respect of the Other's unknown desire to a situation in which the Other wears a mask and the subject never knows what lies behind it. Such a state of "not knowing" gener-ates anxiety. The subject wants to know what he is for the Other and what position he occupies in the Other's discourse. There is, however, another form of anxiety which correlates with the moment when the mask of fantasy fails. In that moment, the subject disappears in the horror of the lack of lack. So the subject accepts (or does not accept) castration as a price to pay in order to be saved from a constant state of anxiety which comes from the Real (Lacan, 1962–63).

Sometimes a warning (per se) may be an intriguing invitation to one subject, but serve as a limit to another. Some might decide to abstain from the embodiment of horror and instead entertain themselves with the tickle. It can be enjoyable to refrain and be amused at a distance from the source of the uncanny. The haunting experience could be made tolerable through a (sexual) fantasy or through certain hobbies. For example, some might opt to enjoy Gothic theme stories or thrillers, at a safe distance from the full-on horror genre. There is, however, another modal-ity of enjoyment that accounts for how some of us are entertained by artworks on a horror theme. We experience the excitement somewhere in the body. It is the same fascination that is felt by lovers of super-high-speed twists and turns in motorsports, or when free-jumping from high altitudes and amusement park rides, in freak-shows that cause the audience fear and anxiety, and also in some sexual practices. The effect of drugs or painful bodily practices can also generate an excitation at the level of the body. The body reacts to such encounters in various ways: physical and mental excitement, euphoria or even in the form of absolute deadness. This, indeed, is what a *symptom* in neurosis is formed for. It protects the subject against a savage attack of *jouissance* in the body, as is encountered quite commonly in some psychotics after a triggered psychosis. In other words, a symptom indexes the Real of *jouissance*.

In Lacan's work, the modality of jouissance which is situated between the Imaginary and the Real rings of the Borromean knot is called *Other jouissance*. Unlike *phallic jouissance*, which is directed towards the object *a* in relation to the Other's desire, Other jouissance goes beyond the Other of language. Phallic jouissance is a form of jouissance correlated to a minus, a lack or a lost object which is sought after indefinitely. Other jouissance is experienced outside the law of language in the body. It is not channelled or directed towards an object. It has an excessive and imprudent nature. This modality of jouissance can occasionally be very troubling for some subjects, requiring them to fight back against it. A patient of mine, mourning her late father, once told me how she had felt nothing of her body and had lost all of her physical sensations while lying down in a bath for a few minutes, an experience that had left her in severe distress. Or, in another case, a patient suffering from sudden black-out attacks would wake from sleep and be fully aware, yet be unable feel the presence of her body and limbs for a few long minutes. This unresponsiveness of her own body had upset her so much that the fear of re-experiencing it had led her to seek help. The uncanniness of it had left her feeling lost and dreadfully alienated. In all the years of my clinical practice, I have never come across a single case of a panic attack in a patient without physical symptoms. In some cases, the patients had searched for a physical cause of their distress.

On the other hand, patients suffering from a bodily illness often complain of anxiety linked to the question of mortality – not only the mortality of their body, but a specific subjective mortality. A bodily disability or impairment can place a limitation on their unique mode of being in the language. This can certainly be tackled or changed by the subject of the unconscious, if there is a strong desire to do so.

In this chapter, we will elaborate the concepts of Other jouissance and the Real body in psychoanalysis.

Which other?

Jouissance is, in fact, a rather confusing term originating from the French verb "jouir" meaning "to enjoy". It is used to describe a psychoanalytical concept in both French and English with connotations of sex and excess which goes beyond any symbolisation. It is experienced as delight. We might tend to talk about such excessive excitement with humour and restraint. It is spoken about under the breath or between the lines. We talk "about" it, "around" it while all knowing how it feels. Based on the Lacanian conceptualisation, jouissance is not simply an affect or the drive; nor is it a pleasurable satisfaction. Excitement – or even deadness – of the body may be as far as language can go to describe the term. Desire and the symptom, besides our ability to rationalise and articulate the sensation (the support of the Imaginary), are the defences against experiencing a morbid jouissance, which is a radical form of non-existence in the language, a certain excessive liveliness (or deadness) that cannot be tolerated if it lasts for long. In other words, desire and the symptom are two types of defence that are in place for neurotics against a savage jouissance. As long as the jouissance is turned into a support of a subject's mode of being, fuelling his desire and symptom, he is somehow safeguarded against this wild form of jouissance attacking his mind and body. This manageable modality of jouissance would be phallic jouissance, which also makes a subject appreciate his liveliness (being alive).

Lacan in his later work suggests that phallic jouissance originates from the field of the Other of language, while Other jouissance originates from the field of the Other of the body. If the drive, according to Lacan, is the reward for the sacrifice that a barred subject makes, at a sexual level, Other jouissance is an invitation to the Real of sexuality between two bodies, each seeking enjoyment independently from one another. Other jouissance does not simply trick or transgress the pleasure principle; it does not merely target "the Thing". It goes beyond any measured phallic value, beyond the limitations of phallic jouissance. It is outside both meaning and the signifier, but not outside the body as the first Other for a subject. It is felt as a mysterious event in the body and is not oriented or directed towards an object (the *objet a*).

From his twentieth seminar onwards, the concept of jouissance in Lacan's work became a game-changer for how we understand the theory of the symptom and the subject of the unconscious. The symptom, instead of being considered as a signifier (as previously in Lacan's work) was theorised as an effect of the Symbolic on the Real of jouissance, at the level of the body. In other words, the symptom translates the unconscious material into Real jouissance. In fact, Lacan moved away from the properties of language towards a focus on the liveliness of a subject's body. Likewise, from this time, instead of focusing on the concept of the subject from a linguistic perspective, he follows up the concept of a subject between language and jouissance, developing a theory of subjectivity through what he calls "parlêtre" (Lacan, 1972–73).

What is a body?

What is a subject's body in psychoanalysis? What would we have become – as humans – if we were born into an immortal body or a body, which does not age and become decrepit?

In psychoanalysis, the subject of the unconscious is not a subject without a living body. A subject might suffer from his memories (actively remembered or encountered unconsciously), but the mortal body can also generate suffering. The subject is not purely and solely the effect of a signifier in the domain of language. The clinic of psychoanalysis attests to this fact when bodily symptoms or complaints are presented to the analyst, or when we observe how a certain narrative induces pain and suffering at the level of the body. So the type of subjectivity that we understand in the domain of psychoanalysis is a bodily event. The psychoanalytical body and bodily events are what we now need to discuss.

It is common knowledge among analysts that the effect of early narratives – before and after a subject's birth – leaves a mark on the social bond between the subject and the Other. Such marks cannot be excluded from bodily events. When a subject investigates his early personal history in order to find out about his place in the Other's desire, there are usually narratives found around his first few words, first steps, teething or, for example, his first haircut. All of these give a reference to the body or a bodily experience. In other words, the narratives are shaped around bodily changes. On the other hand, before the acquisition of language and its properties, the subject had been dealing with another Other: his own body with its needs to survive and grow, and its urges. The needs and excitations, which surprise the child and can cause him discomfort, are newly experienced and need to be dealt with through the interventions of the care giver. The Other of the body has a life of its own that has to be mastered by the subject of the unconscious and that is inevitably affected by the Other's discourse.

Firstly, let us examine the meaning of the Imaginary body. Bodily homeostasis, which fundamentally pursues a survival mode, relies on all of the living organs and systems, with all of the precise physiological process that they involve, in order to maintain the overall equilibrium of the body. All of those bodily events, some involving growth and others decay, signify an underlying order, committed to a single end: to survive. All of the hormonal and neuro-transmitter changes in a human body, with their effect on mood and behaviour, and the bodily urges for sexual intercourse can be understood in the realm of the Imaginary body. This is the body, which is scrutinised, researched and studied in medicine. A place can also be found in this concept of the body for the mind, as the function of the brain that is studied in the realm of psychology.

In psychoanalysis, however, we discuss other aspects of the body. The first encounter of a subject with the image of his body in the mirror phase in the presence of the Other's gaze is the point from which the subject starts to form his mode of being. In the mirror phase the Imaginary body meets the effects of the Symbolic order. This is the point at which the body is subjectified, allowing the subject of the unconscious to come into existence and start his journey of formation. This body of a man or woman in human society lives under the influence of the Other's discourse. The Other of language, which pre-exists the arrival of the subject in the world, introduces a structure and localisation of the libido in the body. The Other of language (of the signifier) mediates between jouissance and the living body of a subject. In other words, language mediates the introduction of jouissance to the body, which is not merely an empty shell or an image. Submission to the signifier of the phallus (as an empty metaphor) at the level of language organises the overwhelming jouissance and creates a minus, enabling the subject to obtain an accessible form of jouissance (phallic jouissance) and enjoy being alive while knowing that he has a mortal body. A lack or minus corresponding to this form of jouissance allows the subject to fashion a desire. The lack of such submission makes some psychotic subjects experience their body as a radical otherness or to feel their body as being occasionally under attack from outside.

Another effect of language on the body is the arrangement of the drive. Jouissance returns to the body in the form of the drive, allowing the subject to gain some sort of pleasure (as a reward for the sacrifice made in a compromise between his sexuality and civilisation) through the medium of the body. Here, we have another concept for understanding the meaning of the body: the concept of the

Real body, the body as a "medium" to experience enjoyment at the level of the drive rather than of the instincts. Excess and repetition are the characteristics of these experiences. The body with its "smart" homeostasis, physio-pathological conditions and an image for the subject of the unconscious, now offers him an enjoyment accessed through a subjective arrangement of the drive. The Other of language plays a fundamental role in forming such an arrangement. The drive is, in fact, a concept that goes as far as anything in Freud's work can go to help us understand the Real body in psychoanalysis. In Lacan's work on the Borromean knot, the Real body is at the heart of his conceptualisation of the subject (parlêtre), symptom and jouissance. The Real body is the body which bears the marks of language on jouissance. From the mirror phase onwards, the body has an image, is objectified and is cared for. Thereafter it is discourse, which conditions the living body in social bonds. The Real body escapes discourse and encounters jouissance independently. It is the symptom (if it is formed) as a bodily event, which makes jouissance accessible for a subject via the drive. In psychoanalysis, the body is given life not only and not merely because of its organic homeostasis but as the locus where a subject starts his formation. Without a body there shall be no subject and vice versa. In this respect, we are born dead and in order to be brought to life, our body is gradually conditioned to bear the effect of language on its jouissance. A subject does not simply own his body but has to claim it. The first effort to claim/subjectify the body starts with guess work aimed at the mother tongue: an opaque state in which a subject is called on to carve out a position and form a way to carry on living. This way/symptom can be altered later in life, but its existence is essential to enables a subject to come to life/being.

Pain and the real body

In medicine the question of life and death (mortality) in a human being has a very clear answer. The body has a smart system to maintain its homeostasis or to start off the death process towards the end of a subject's life. In other words, medicine seems to have a straightforward answer to the question of mortality. In psychoanalysis, the concept of the subject includes a mortal body which is both objectified and subjectified in the three dimensions of the Imaginary, Symbolic and Real. Therefore, the question of life and death (mortality) concerns the subject as well as concerning an organic body, which has both a life and its own arrangements in respect of enjoyment. This is why, we cannot follow the same logic in psychoanalysis as in medicine when approaching the question of mortality. The body in medicine is rather understood as the Imaginary body, and it is admitted that there are many unknown causes for bodily changes. In psychoanalysis, the concepts of subject and body are intertwined and cannot be approached separately. The birth and formation of the subject and his agency in fashioning a particular mode of being is not understood without the Other of the body. On the other hand, the subject's approach to the Other of the body, who seeks pleasure (sometimes in excess), can influence the health and illness of the body. If the nature of our organic body was different, the formation of the subject would certainly be affected. We have formed our mode of being in language with the question of the mortal body. If we could live for a much longer (or much shorter) time or be immortal, would our subjectivity be different? It certainly would. Let us take an example from the cinema to elaborate on this question:

In the *Westworld* series, a re-creation of a 1970s film with the same title, the bodies of the so-called "hosts" – androids at a theme park, on which paying guests act out their (sometimes erotic or violent) fantasies – do not follow the same rules as an organic body. They are made in the lab, can be replaced, modified or repaired. These hosts do not age. They have not experienced an organic birth, which is the first traumatic experience of human beings. They have come to life at a certain age, repeating a loop scenario. Eventually, one of them manages to solve the "maze", leading to awareness (sentience) of their inception and the role they are designed to carry out. Their creator had designed the maze as a possibility, by which the hosts would be able to set themselves free and choose a life purpose that suited them. In particular, they would be able to make a choice: to stay or to leave the Westworld park. In this context, what in the series is called "sentience" is a close enough analogy to subjective agency in psychoanalysis. It is an ability to interpret the ambiguous mother tongue into whatever meaning a subject can make of his being and then to form (or not to form) a symptom based on this initial interpretation. The symptom is equated with a life purpose for each subject of the unconscious.

The concept of the body and subjectivity presented and dealt with in the clinic of psychoanalysis is situated between the Symbolic and the Real rings of the Borromean knot. Likewise, in the Westworld scenario, the Imaginary aspect of the body is minimised and the main focus is on the Symbolic and Real body. Each host's body is a home to a new role in a different theme or narrative in the park. In the main theme of this fictional scenario, the body is a structure where a host's internal core (the pearl) is placed in or can be replaced. Moreover, the fact that each host's core is transferable to another body of a new generation of robots can indicate the trans-generational continuity of a discourse. This pattern may remind us of the effect of a certain discourse/culture on the Symbolic body of the subject of the unconscious.

On the other hand, the pain experienced by the hosts, the fear of death (signalling the question of mortality), all sorts of suffering they face, such as loss and grief, their bodily dysfunctionality, can all be understood as the Real aspect of the body. Here, the idea of pain plays two roles: pain referred to as a host's cornerstone, motivating them to go through life (similar to the function of a subject's symptom), and pain as a precondition for the host to take action on their true desire. Bernard, a host character in the Westworld park, was left with the pain of grief over his dead child. This pain acted as his cornerstone/symptom: "this pain is all I am left with". This form of pain can be understood as a morbid jouissance induced by a dysfunctional symptom. To leave Westworld the hosts need to suffer more in order to be able to make a choice. The choice, here, is how far a subject is willing and ready to go through his pain (being a programmed host) in order to fulfil and act upon his desire.

Pain, from a psychoanalytical perspective, is where a subject transgresses and tends to go beyond the pleasure principle. The Freudian death drive and Lacan's earlier work on the concept of jouissance approached the question of psychical pain beyond sensory perception. However, being in pain can also be a symptom – as in the Westworld scenario, acting as a proxy against subjective mortality. In other words, the pain is a marker of being alive. For example in a couple relationship, the experience of physical or psychical pain can be a symptom that protects against the impossible reality of the sexual non-rapport between two bodies.

In a couple that I came to know of in my practice, a person who was suffering from bodily pain, manifested through various physical illnesses and eating problems, was taken care of and loved through being nursed. Facing the idea that one partner might not be almost constantly ill seemed to be impossible for both of them. What would remain for them to relate to if the patient-nurse scenario came to an end? This became their question to work through in the direction of the treatment. In another couple, grief over a dead child had taken a significant place in their relationship. The pain of grief was the cornerstone of their relationship. This position towards the pain of loss had given a structure to their relationship, which had created a path in life for each of them.

Hence, we see how a pain symptom can offer certain possibilities for a sexual non-rapport between two Real bodies.

Autumn Sonata, a film by Ingmar Bergman, focuses on a mother-daughter relationship. While the mother character had formed here own way of coping with feelings arising from sexual non-rapport with her partners, the daughter had made the pain of her grief over her child's death into the cornerstone of her relationship with her husband. Moreover, her impossible relationship with her mother, had made her a different woman in life. She cared for her disabled sister, who seemed to be abandoned by her mother.

As we discussed in the chapter on symptom formation, a subject can find his symptom on a lack or shortcoming in the mode of being of the previous generation. Such a lack is, in fact, a precondition for forming a symptom. Facing and then doing something with this lack generates pain and suffering. Here, pain can be understood as an exchange currency between being stuck in an opaque jouissance or setting oneself free from such morbid jouissance (the fabric of the Real).

In other words, pain can be a precondition for a subject to feel alive. For a child, bearing the pain of recognising a lack in the Other as well as the pain of accepting that he is not cable of filling that Symbolic lack, can be a substitute for the constant horror of dealing with the opacity of a morbid jouissance. If such a trade happens, where the pain of loss (not being capable of making good the Other's lack) is substituted for the painful and haunting experience of morbid jouissance, we have the structure of a neurosis. Otherwise, as it is evident in the clinic of psychosis, the overwhelming pain of being stuck in the fabric of the Real makes the subject's life a constant struggle. In perversion, the pain of being, expressed through rage and anguish, is due to being stuck in a fantasy of being the sinthome/ the one/the epicentre of the world. The perverse subject may be unable to bear not being "the one" for the Other. Lacan (following Freud) calls this "disavowal" – disavowing knowledge about someone's lack as castration, while at the same time knowing that such a lack exists. Instead of the exchange that we see in neurosis between the pain of recognising the Other's lack and the pain of doing something with this lack, in perversion there is no exchange and the perverse subject chooses to be the pain, the horror behind the mask. In other words, the perverse subject's ego equates with the sinthome (Soler, 2018). Or, he might become the sinthome which generates pain, fear and anguish in the Other.

Moreover, in any psychical structure that we discuss in the clinic of psychoanalysis, the pain of what to do with the Other of the body, which seeks pleasure independently, has to come to terms with the social bond. Each subject of the unconscious, who is doomed to be a speaking being, will have to endure pain in order to break through the silence of a primary opaque jouissance and bring his body into life while bearing the marks of culture. Otherwise, the body remains as a dead cage where the subject is imprisoned, or even has never had the chance to burgeon as a subject of the unconscious, as we see in many cases of autism. As discussed in the chapter on diagnosis, disconnection from primary jouissance, in whatever way or by whatever strategy, may return to the subject as an overwhelming state of jouissance if a similar scenario is repeated at the level of the fantasy.

The real body and the clinic

In the clinic of neurosis we may encounter a physical illness or a physical irritation that affects the body. Such an illness can be the result of a translation, which a symptom imposes on the body from a subjective interpretation. Other jouissance is experienced in the form of a bodily event (excitation or deadness) outside any structure of the Symbolic. Such an excitation originates from the opaque holes of the Real in the Symbolic. In the moment of experiencing it, the subject of the unconscious disappears. Lacan made increasing use of the term "parlêtre" towards the end of his teaching. A parlêtre comes to life as a result of the Real effect of language on the body, which has its own agency in obtaining enjoyment. Other jouissance is the manifestation of the Real effect of language on the body while also being an expression of the Real body.

This approach to the concept of *symptom*, *subject* and *jouissance* in Lacan's later theories has certainly had consequences in the clinic. Some clinicians might mistake a symptom for Other jouissance. This can be one explanation, in some cases, of clinical mis-diagnosis or of difficulty in making a differential diagnosis. The manifestation of Other jouissance in a female psychotic patient may be interpreted as a neurotic symptom. Or, conversely, Other jouissance in the clinic of a neurotic can be mistaken for a psychotic phenomenon, as an invasion of his mode of being from the Real.

Other jouissance (or feminine jouissance) at the level of the Real body was a concept in Lacan's theories referring to a subject's enjoyment of sexuality beyond the phallus. Bodily excitation and deadness can be both horrifying and enjoyable in a subject regardless of psychical structural differences. It is usually in the clinic of psychosis that we hear an account of such bodily experiences, but they can also exist in neurotic analysands. In psychosis, however, the problem of how to deal with such phenomena can occasionally become extremely acute. Our argument regarding Other jouissance (felt as a bodily excitation) is best illustrated through clinical examples.

Case A

Ms. R contacted me soon after breaking up with her partner, seeking help with unbearable anxiety. A request for more details revealed that one possible source of the anxiety was her experience of sharp pains below her chest. The location of the pain was specific and described by her as a typical sign of her anxiety. Much detailed elaboration of her past in relation to her pain and anxiety followed, in both abstract and precise terms. She said that she had had a similar pain earlier in life, at the age of around 5 or 6, when her father left the family home. One specialist judged that the child's reported pain was imaginary, but a surgeon who did not want to risk overlooking the possibility of a life-threatening appendicitis in a young child carried out an appendectomy. Results from the pathology lab showed no appendicitis. She remembered her maternal grandmother, sitting next to her bed after hearing the result and saying under her breath, "This is the pain of a goodbye", associating R.'s physical pain with her father's departure from the family. After recovering from the operation, Ms. R. had experienced various other episodes of such pain, in all of which a separation from a love object was at stake, echoing her grandmother's words. As an adult, in all her romantic relationships, she had left her partners as soon as she had felt the threat of a breakup, thus avoiding the threat of physical pain. However, in the most recent instance, she had not been able to predict her partner's sudden decision, and the physical pain was the result.

In this case, the "appendectomy" had not – metaphorically – extracted the source of excitation and pain from her body. In her narratives, her grandmother's words at the hospital bed were, in fact, given significant space and agency. However, this naming had not resulted in any symptom formation on her part. It had not functioned as the cause of a symptom formation as happens in neurosis, where the operation of naming gives an envelope to a symptom, indexing an unbearable mode of jouissance on the body. In the Freudian sense, the appendectomy itself had not functioned as a castrating agent. The subject had not decided to pay the price (castration) in order to be saved from remaining stuck in the primary jouissance. In her case, the pain, which was present before it was called "the pain of a goodbye" did not disappear forever, although the anxiety caused by it was tempered by its naming. The act of naming had functioned as a compass for the subject to organise her distance from the Other, as in her relationships with men. At the level of her symptomology, besides leaving her men and also her places of living (almost constantly), she was fascinated by bodily pain, as inflicted through various sexual and non-sexual practices.

There seemed to be two types of pain in this case: a pain that caused anxiety, which was related to a separation from a significant other and hence, remaining struck in a morbid state of jouissance (primary jouissance), and a pain, which she was in control of and had agency in making into a source of enjoyment. In her case, phallic jouissance was not present. Since her childhood she had often managed to save herself from the blaze of anguish and pain that accompanied a separation, but not always successfully. She had devised a system of being in control of her anxiety in order to exercise agency over her life and choices. In another vignette, she referred to another bodily event in the form of severe dizziness leading to fainting. This occurred in some encounters with others – mainly with love interests who did not seem to be attracted to her. This manifestation was interpreted as a stereotype of hysterical fainting in her narrative. Later in the work, she interpreted her fainting episodes as a way to re-create her early childhood hospitalisation where her father had visited her only shortly and only once.

Her main problem in life was how to avoid "being left behind". "To be left behind" meant for her a painful, uncontrollable irritation in her body. In her case there was no sign of phallic jouissance, of any appreciation of being alive and moving forward in life with the help of a desire. Ms. R. did not seem to have formed any symptom to carry out the task of translating the unconscious letter into the Real body. Unlike a neurotic subject who is somehow saved from the sudden onset of horrifying jouissance by the help of a symptom, she had to constantly invent and test ways of avoiding the attack. In the clinic of neurosis, the motto of "being left behind" can be found in the subject's symptom (as a supporting scenario) and can be expressed as a mysterious excitation on the Real body at the time of a separation from a love object.

The Real body which seeks enjoyment can sometimes be experienced as a real dilemma for the psychotic subject. A patient of mine told me once how not having sexual intercourse for some time had caused such overwhelming excitement all over her body that she had to spend hours in the gym in heavy exercise, to tire herself out. Addiction to vigorous physical exercise (several hours each day) had become, in fact, her means of dealing with the overwhelming jouissance. If, for a neurotic, Other jouissance can offer a mode of access for enjoying a sexual non-rapport, in psychosis it is all that the subject, as a sexed being, is left with, and can come back to their as an attack on the Real body.

Case B

Mr. A had been in analysis for many years before he came to see me. After a break of a few years from his first analysis, he had decided to come back to analysis in order to find out why he had gained so much weight (his weight problem had led to diabetes, which was treated by injections of insulin). The weight gain had happened just over a year after his marriage. Change of eating habits and binging on snacks were the reasons he gave. However, he also noticed that entering into marriage seemed linked to his physical change. He had experienced an episode of numbness all over his body while lying in bed a few weeks after his wedding night. He felt control over his body draining away and his body turning into what felt like dead mass. He felt pinned to the bed. This deadness had lasted for few minutes. Earlier the same evening, he had been celebrating his wife's graduation with family and friends. He and his wife were course mates and he had always helped with her assignments.

The experience of his body on that night was beyond the function of his symptom (being a helper or a tutor) and beyond phallic jouissance (offering a sense of liveliness to him through that role). It had taken him by surprise and marked a moment when the Symbolic was bypassed and the Real of the body was touched in a manner beyond the subject's control. He had suffered from a few more similar episodes. Deadness, heaviness or stagnation in the body were, in fact, significant impositions that coincided with situations of both happiness and distress. He had a potentially life-threatening illness: he was obese and had a coronary stent. Medical intervention was taking care of his body, while offering him bodily excitation through a range of injections and speculations. "Being heavy" was also, later, associated with his mother's description of her labour during his birth. He weighed 7kg (heavy for a new-born) which caused a difficult labour. He had interpreted this particular narrative around his birth in a sense that made his weight a cause of pain to others. His interpretation of the equivocal "heavy birth" had decided that the core of his symptom would be *not* being a burden to others, hence, being a helper. Based on such an interpretation, he had endeavoured to be as quick as he could in finishing his schooling, getting a job that would lead to a career and always being hands-on in helping others (not causing them trouble). Nevertheless, he sometimes experienced his being as heaviness, like that of a dead body.

An experience of deadness of the body offered him jouissance in the form of *Other jouissance* in a space outside the Other of language. It resonated with his symptom (being a helper so that he would not be a heavy burden) and was felt on his Real body. That night of his wife's graduation party, when his role as a tutor seemed to have ended, he had momentarily experienced the return of the Real in the form of bodily deadness. After this episode, which was correlated with a "plus" rather than a "minus" jouissance, in the second analysis, the work continued to speak to the Real body by pushing towards a domain beyond the earlier signification.

Conclusion

Although Other jouissance is often discussed as feminine jouissance, it is found in both male and female subjects and is perhaps better associated with the Real body. It can be manifested as a bodily excitation and as deadness of the body – a jouissance beyond any structure, outside the Symbolic, in the realm of the Real of sexual non-rapport. It reflects the non-rapport between two bodies, since they cannot share such an experience of jouissance. The modality of the *Other jouissance* can be experienced as a bodily event when a subject faces a non-lacking Other, and it can be a haunting experience.

So long as horror is experienced as a touch of the Real through some kind of barrier, it will remain at the level of accessible enjoyment – when, for example, it is experienced through certain sources of fascination in everyday life, as in horror films or literature, or through various practices which involve risk-taking. In other words, the unbearable fear (the horror of an unbarred Other) can only be approached with a mask. After the COVID-19 outbreak, many governments have made it compulsory to use a mask in public places, not so much to prevent the spread of the virus as to encourage people to go out and feel safe. Has this strategy really made the horror of being contaminated or contaminating others more tolerable? Horror is an exposure to the Real of subjective mortality, which a subject wants to know nothing of. Pain is the marker of such an encounter. Being in pain, however, can be a symptom as well as a position (being it). The former is found in the structure of neurosis while the latter indicates a perverse position in the language. In psychosis, due to the lack of phallic jouissance, the very fact of being alive can be painful.

Bibliography

Lacan, J. (1962–3). *The seminar of Jacque Lacan: Book X: Anxiety*. A. R. Price (Trans.). Cambridge: Polity Press.

Lacan, J. (1972–3). *The seminar of Jacque Lacan: Book XX: On feminine sexuality the limits of love and knowledge*. J. A. Miller (Ed.) and B. Fink (Trans.). New York: Norton.

Soler, C. (2018). *Lacan reading Joyce*. Devra Simiu (Trans.). London: Routledge.

Figure 6.1 Growing in the Darkness, photograph by Bardia Moeini

Chapter 6

Feelings

Emotions and feelings in the ancient thought

The modern Persian language – Farsi – has two words with meanings that roughly coincide with the two English words, "emotion" and "feeling". For "emotion" Farsi has "shoor", which carries the sense of excitation (also contained in the English "emotion") while for "feeling" we have "ehsas", which is similar to English in referring to a *state* rather than to excitation. However, both terms are used in modern Persian literature almost interchangeably. "Feeling" refers to what is perceived cognitively and can affect mood. The Persian language also has a diverse and rich lexicon to describe and name different emotions and feelings. The word used for "emotion" can be traced back to texts in ancient Persian languages: Old Avestan, Younger Avestan and Elamite. But, like Aristotle's list of ancient Greek names for the "emotions", the ancient Persian words that name and describe different emotions and feelings are far more limited than the elaborate range of words in modern Farsi. Also, in ancient texts one finds a clear dualistic division between pleasant and unpleasant feelings, rather than a distinction of each based on a specific description.

"Eros" in ancient Greek covered the meanings of "love" and "emotion". The Middle-Persian language (Pahlavi), which succeeded the Elamite language of the Persian Empire and preceded modern Farsi, had a word that is close to "eros": the Pahlavi "mehr" stands for love, desire, goodness, friendship, kindness and also the sun. It is believed that the term originates from a time before Zoroastrianism and was associated with ancient Mithraism, a religion that was born in what is now Iran and that inspired the Mithraic mysteries, which rivalled Christianity in the late-Roman empire. Mithraism and Zoroastrianism are the first specifically Persian contributions to world religion and thought, to be followed by Manichaeism, Mazdakism and Zurvanism, all prior to the arrival in Persia of Islam, brought by Arab invaders about 1400 years ago.

Plato, who took the soul to have three parts – appetite, spirit and reason, attached Eros to each part of the soul in a different way. Appetite was the seat of sex, greed and promiscuity, while spirit was associated with control of appetite and was the seat of anger and shame. The high level of reason (wisdom and rationality) was

DOI: 10.4324/9781003184799-7

linked with the love of knowledge and with true happiness, the idea being that love of wisdom results in true happiness. Unlike Plato, Aristotle thought that the human soul has two parts: the logical and the a-logical. He placed the emotions in the a-logical part of the soul. He was the first western philosopher to theorise the emotions and he introduced the idea of catharsis (cleansing) of the soul. Greek tragedy and comedy were considered to be cathartic practices, which allowed the subject to experience different emotions and feelings as the drama unfolded.

The earliest texts from ancient Persia are the *Gathas* – the poems of Zoroaster, the founder of Zoroastrianism. In his poems, philia (a Greek word), as a form of non-sexual love, is expressed in the form of care and protection of other humans as well as other natural beings in the world. In Zoroaster's doctrine, humans are the guardians of nature – the protectors of water, air, fire and earth. In the *Gathas* the symbols of light and darkness, rather than being external forces inflicted upon the subject, are metaphors for the subject's own internal temptation/excitation. Eros is also referred to an inner, guiding light. Mithraism and Zoroastrianism call for the worship of wisdom as that which guides the subject towards Eros (light and truth). The term "worship" conveys the bestowing of absolute love with honour. So, the highest form of love (Eros) is linked with absolute truth and knowledge.

Feelings and emotions in ancient Persian literature

What treatments of emotions do we find in the ancient Persian world?

The earliest surviving texts, dating from the Achaemenid dynasty and written in the Elamite language, are the Cyrus cylinder (created in 539 BCE) and two inscriptions found in Behistun and Persepolis in the North-West and the South of modern Iran.

In the Cyrus Cylinder, the great kings of Persia declare their triumph over their rivals and their aspiration to maintain peace through the love of and devotion to Ahura Mazda, the God of light and wisdom. In the Behistun inscription, which is not a work of literature but a King's declaration, Darius the Great takes pride in coming of a family that was noble since antiquity and declares that such nobility has legitimised his right to the throne and, hence, his right to suppress rebellions. From a psychoanalytic perspective, King Darius's powerful suppression of his rivals (after the death of Cyrus the Great) is a manifestation of the emotion of envy rather than of greed. Envy between rivals can be settled through the application of justice. In these texts, we find the King's justification and legitimation of his claim to the kingdom and the throne, and his claim to have the blessing of Ahura Mazda (the God of light and wisdom) on his peaceful reign.

Besides the declarations of Cyrus and Darius, the principal surviving work from Ancient Persia is the *Gathas* – a collection of ancient poems believed to have been written by Zoroaster, and the first work of Persian literature. The *Gathas* are 17 hymns written in the ancient language of Persia: Old Avestan. It is believed that the love of knowledge and truth in Zoroastrianism had substantial influence on ancient Greek and Roman philosophy. In particular, the "worship of wisdom" (Mazda Yasna) in Ancient Persia is equated with "love of knowledge" in Greek philosophy. Indeed, the content of the *Gathas* is more philosophical than religious. Zoroaster's poems are addressed to the lord of wisdom (Ahura Mazda) as well as to his people. In Zoroastrianism, Ahura Mazda is the all-knowing God who is the representative of absolute light and wisdom. The mission of Zoroaster was to search for the absolute truth, and it is in the search for this absolute truth that happiness can be attained. We can infer that wisdom (Mazda) in Zoroaster's *Gathas*, is, in fact, absolute truth rather than simply a human virtue, although, in Zoroastrian doctrine (religion), Mazda is a subject's capacity for dealing with the force of self-destruction (akin to Freud's "Thanatos" – the death drive).

The development of language and social change during the history of civilisation has complicated the question of "wisdom" and "judgment" in relation to the system of pleasure and pain. As psychoanalysts we should be particularly interested by this question: Does the Zoroastrian worship of wisdom (Mazda Yasna) coincide with the Greek and Roman Stoic philosophy by showing how a subjective, cognitive judgment can transform an unpleasant feeling into a pleasant feeling? Zoroaster's poems refer to wisdom as a knowledge or truth (Yasna), which is worshipped. In the love and honour accorded to an absolute truth, Persian culture is making this truth an agent, which causes the subject's desire to search for it throughout his or her life. This device may well remind us of the Lacanian *object a*. The promise of salvation (happiness) depends on a practice of seeking for absolute truth or knowledge and this practice can transform pain into pleasure or happiness. Isn't this another way of saying that wisdom or wise judgment is just a subject's "agency" in choosing his or her journey in life as being (or not being) the journey of the search for truth? By choosing this journey the subject is protected against his own tendency towards self-destruction. Just as Freud (and, after him, Lacan) believed in desire as a rampart against the excessiveness in the drive, absolute truth (Mazda) motivates and guides the wisest men and women to a search, by which they create their own ethics. Zoroastrianism views this as the best way of life.

Another emotion that is addressed in the *Gathas* is Zoroaster's "doubt" – either an unpleasant feeling induced by his doubts or his doubts themselves as an unpleasant feeling, which led him to seek knowledge from the holder of all truth, Ahura Mazda. He addresses his sense of helplessness in his own community and asks for guidance and blessing for himself, so that he would not remain in a state of constant doubt concerning his existence in his community. The *Gathas* pose rhetorical questions about the best way of life and enjoyment and propose some answers: searching for truth guarantees enjoyment in life, the greatest good is the desire for truth, and a pivotal role is given to human intellect and thought centred on ethics. Zoroaster's poetry promotes the worship of wisdom. The best form of thought (the "Good Thought"), according to the *Gathas*, is to desire truth and avoid self-deception. Zoroaster begins from Ahura Mazda as the primal father or creator of the truth and ends with human intellect as the place where the search for truth is pursued. The love of knowledge, for Zoroaster, is not simply a therapeutic philosophy, as Epicurus or later Stoic philosophy might suggest: to be the searcher for truth and knowledge is a calling and a destiny, which defines the desirable mode of being. Seeds of doubt that cause him pain and suffering make Zoroaster question his existence as a social being in his community. He is separated from his tribe and goes into a self-imposed exile. Zoroaster eventually returns to his community with what Lacan would call his "sinthome": his *Gathas* and a school of thought (Good Thoughts, Good Words and Good Deeds). In his poems, he encourages his followers to question and search for the truth – as Socrates did in Ancient Greece – and to fashion their own rational ethics. Philosophy was a personal consolation for Zoroaster as it was for the Roman philosopher, Boethius (author of the *Consolation of Philosophy*). This is in contrast with the idea that "searching for truth" is interpreted as telling the truth and doing good in the world.

Another emotion found in the *Gathas* is that of sadness. In the Avestan language, sadness, unpleasant emotion and pain are expressed by a term that literally means "weeping". In the last part of the *Gathas*, Zoroaster tells his followers that, in order to reach the blessing of happiness, they need to endure a period of suffering and pain. The way to embark on such a journey of discovery is to endure pain. Paradoxically, then, suffering pain is part and parcel of the pleasure to be obtained by the achievement of truthful knowledge.

In the *Avesta*, the religious book of Zoroastrians, the God of Destruction is Angra Mainyu (Ahriman) who is evil by choice and who will be destroyed at the end of the world. The term "Angra Mainyu" in old Avestan means chaos, destruction, death as well as anger or rage. Such destructive temptation always appears in disguise and works to obstruct the search for truth. So that which fights against the truth is deceptive, false and a lie. In Zoroastrian doctrine, an individual is never entirely safe from this demonic temptation. The Zoroastrian religious doctrine holds that a person can manage their anger by using clear judgment and reason. However, "wisdom" in Zoroastrian philosophy is a matter of personal ethics. It is not merely the management of anger, but also the ability to reject temptation. Such temptation (the Freudian death drive or Lacanian jouissance) is expressed through feeling in the form of anger or sadness and is experienced as an excitation. Movement towards the truth (light) or, on the contrary, towards self-destruction depends on the subject's choice, i.e., on wisdom. In the terms of a philosophical theory of the emotions, anger and sadness can be taken to be "motivating emotions".

Ahura Mazda and Ahriman, the key spirits or gods of Zoroastrianism, have much in common, then, with the life and death drives of psychoanalysis. Various myths with protagonists deriving from Ahura Mazda and Ahriman can be found in Persian literature after the *Gathas*, notably in Ferdowsi's epic poem, *Shahnameh* (The Book of Kings), which is the earliest extended text in the Persian language, written around one thousand years ago. *Shahnameh* gives a romanticised account of the history of Persia, with an abundance of mythical personages, symbols and metaphors. The language is highly emotional, expressing states that range from euphoric happiness to the deepest grief. Ferdowsi's book revived Persian language and pre-Islamic culture after the Arab invasions (*Shahnameh* was written about 400 years after the Islamic conquest of Iran).

In the Book of Kings, Ferdowsi mythologises evil as an external presence in the universe, which eventually acquires an internal presence in the family structure. Firstly, the evil finds expression in the envy of two brothers towards their third brother, who is loved and honoured by their father. Envy originates from a family drama and leads to a desperate struggle on the battlefield.

The second exploration of envy and sexual desire in *Shahnameh* is set in the court of the Shah. The Shah's wife, Sudabeh, passionately desires her step-son, Siyavash, who rejects her advances. Infuriated, she kills another woman – a mother of twins – in order to conceal her passion and incriminate Siyavash. The young man proves his innocence on this occasion, but eventually perishes. The story of Siyavash has played an important role in the history of Iranian culture for more than a thousand years. Some writers have treated the tragic death of Siyavash as a symbol of national grief and the story has marked the Shiite tradition in Islam, which is centred on the martyrdom of a holy man.

Jealousy or envy in *Shahnameh* can be in the form of rivalry over temporal power or of sexual jealousy and the urge to possession in love. In the story of Siyavash and other epic tales in *Shahnameh*, three other main emotions are described, namely anger, shame and grief. Anger leads to violence and murder (as an act of revenge), shame (exposure to the gaze of the Other) entails the loss of one's honour, while grief is experienced in the loss of a loved one. Grief is well depicted in the death of Siyavash (brought about by court intrigues) and the story of Jawira (the first wife of Siyavash) who loses her son, Foroud, in battle. She tears her stomach open while cradling the body of her son, who she had loved more than anybody else and who was her sole purpose in life (her symptom). After Siyavash's death, his second wife, Farangis, who was passionately in love with him, raises their son, Kai Khosrow, and accompanies him to war in order to avenge the death of Siyavash. Here, grief is a "motivating" emotion, dealt with either through an acting-out (as with Jawira) or by its translation into revenge.

The revenge theme is also apparent in another principal character in the *Shahnameh* stories – Rostam, who trained and nurtured Siyavash to become a knight. His grief over Siyavash's death is turned into violent revenge. He kills Sudabeh, the passionate lover of Siyavash, whom he blames for Siyavash's unfortunate destiny (exile and death). Rostam also kills his own son, Sohrab, failing to recognise the young soldier as his nearest relative and jealous of the younger man's strength. Ferdowsi writes that Rostam's arrogance and lust for power blind him in this episode, and his emotions are transformed from envy and anger to unbearable shame and grief when he discovers the identity of the man he has killed.

At the end of *Shahnameh*, Rostam, himself is deceived and killed together with his remarkable horse, Rakhsh, due to the envy and grudge of his half-brother, Shaghad. In Persian popular culture Shaghad's malicious envy of his own brother is due to his birth from a different mother, expressing the idea that the essence and nature of the child originate from the mother's milk. The Persian legend also suggests that the essence of a subject cannot be changed or transformed by what Plato calls rationality and wisdom. The mother's milk, as the fabric of the Real, can be seen as the ambiguous mother tongue, from which a subject forms a signification, carving a space for himself in language.

The three dominant emotions in Ferdowsi's epic – anger, shame and grief – combine into a state of feeling that amounts to anguish.

Persian thought in the Islamic era

The first Persian thinker of the Islamic era is the philosopher Avicenna, whose ideas are based on Aristotle and the Neo-Platonic approach to the soul, reason, the rational and choice. The human soul, according to Avicenna, is an organising principle and the seat of emotions. Following the example of Aristotle in ancient Greece, Avicenna is the first Persian philosopher to theorise the emotions. He believed that emotions have various components and create motivational power for a subject, moving him forward in life and generating apprehension. Avicenna believed that emotions are divided into two groups – pleasant and unpleasant – and that it is in humans, due to their awareness of time and memories, that the sense of fear and hope exist. Humans have *rational* souls, unlike the souls of animals and vegetables, and our rational souls are able to evaluate situations in order to decide on the appropriate emotion towards the relevant object, depending on whether it is the cause of pleasure or displeasure. Anxiety and a sense of the uncanny in humans are not a result of instinctual experiences. Emotions, for Avicenna, have a cognitive core. They involve feelings, they suggest certain behavioural pattern and have effects on the body.

Avicenna was a doctor of medicine and his thinking was focused on the effect of emotions on physical health and disease. He introduced the concept of psychosomatic illnesses, in which psychological disturbances can influence the homeostasis of the body. Besides physical health, he gave a central role to the "rational" as the main element of control over psychological health. He believed, for example, that mood disorder originates from humidity in the brain and that hyper-ventilation can increase the sense of happiness. If black bile (one of the four humours) is dominant in the body, the patient will suffer from melancholy. Avicenna took phobia to be an extreme form of fear and avoidance (akin to melancholia) while anger was the dominant emotion in mania.

Another philosopher, Suhrawardi, led the Persian revival of Platonism and Neo-Platonism. According to Henry Corbin, French philosopher and Iranologist, Suhrawardi's philosophy, as a philosophy of "illumination", represents a restoration of ancient Persian wisdom. As already discussed, the Zoroastrian wisdom, based on the *Gathas* is a search for the absolute truth, the light which can lead a subject towards salvation and happiness. Suhrawardi takes Hermes Trismegistus, the purported author of Egyptian philosophical texts, and Socrates to have been the true "founders" of philosophy while Plato was the "master" or a "skilful teacher" of philosophy. Illumination philosophy intertwines knowledge with subjective intuition (feeling) and has three levels: intuitive, observational and illuminative. Intuitive knowledge is valued above theoretical knowledge since the former generates further knowledge and inspires a passion for life in the subject. Suhrawardi's philosophy is not simply a consolation but a mode of life. His ideas on emotions and feelings run contrary to Avicenna's emphasis on the relationship between emotions and bodily perception, the imagination and the production of memories.

After Suhrawardi, the emotions are further elaborated in the thought of Mulla Sadra, who theorised them as forms of "passion" or "excitation". Certain emotions, such as anger, fear and lust are linked to the non-divine aspect of a subject and a true intellectual being is someone whose feelings are free from those temptations. True wisdom is inseparable from divine love, according to Mulla Sadra. The best, "elite" form of existence is one that is full of passion for divine love and this state cannot be reached without the cleansing of the soul from unwise and mortal (non-divine) emotions, such as anger, fear and sexual temptation. However, Mulla Sadra believed that some earthly love relationships can be nurtured and led towards divine love and knowledge or wisdom. The "rational" has a central role in this philosophy as a way of controlling anger and lust, which are the two principal emotions that can prevent a subject from reaching divine truth. The rational has the role of moderator and the idea of sublimation of emotions into a passionate, divine love is much discussed by Mulla Sadra. But if emotional temptations, such as doubt or lust, are to be elevated to help the subject reach a higher love (divinity), they must be endorsed and carefully nurtured. Mulla Sadra takes thought, emotions and feelings to be motivational forces that can lead to cognitive activities.

Sufism, which is a specifically Persian Islamic mysticism, views the soul as tripartite, consisting of wisdom (spirit), self and heart with wisdom as a barrier between the heart and the dark, instinctual self. The higher level of soul is the "spirit" which is supposed to surround the will of the individual in the interest of the will of God. The heart is the moderator of emotions and source of love oneself. The ego (self) in Sufi philosophy is autocratic and controlled by sexual desire in the form of lust. The emotions associated with the self are tyranny (cruelty) and regret, which can potentially be purified into inspiration and serenity through reason. In the Sufi model of the soul, the place of knowledge, intellect and wisdom is the heart, so that "intuitive" knowledge has a higher level than abstract, given facts and theoretical knowledge. So, the rational in Sufism is in contrast with Aristotelian logical reason. The purpose of life in Sufism is to reach the highest level of being, where happiness is attained by strengthening and finding a balance in oneself. The subject is then able to love others by virtue of a compassionate heart. Happiness, therefore, is not reached by means of the rational intellect but through the heart and by way of a course of pain and suffering. So the approach of Sufism to happiness and serenity differs from that of the Stoics who believed that rational judgment affects the way in which an individual endures hardship in order to have an easier life in society. The Sufi approach to happiness is also in contrast with that of Mulla Sadra, who gave a central role to reason in the control of anger and raw passion. Seclusion in Sufism is a way of obtaining unity with absolute love through deep reflection and contemplation. This means that the subject becomes ready (or not) to honour sincerity as well as being truthful with their emotions. The logic here is to face pain (the most real feeling) and eventually transform anger, violence, hatred, paranoia and doubts into compassionate, divine love. The particularity of each subject in reaching a personal truth and of the way in which unity with this truth is attained is well recognised in Sufism. The emotions are neither denied, nor disappear, but are transformed from raw passion into desire in the form of longing and affection for a higher, absolute soul. Emotions in Sufism are motivational and goal-oriented.

Psychoanalytical affects

When someone experiences an unexpected, unpleasant feeling – this could be sadness, grief, fear, anger, irritation, agitation or stress – in the actual moment the emotion is expressed, he will not make any attempt to figure out its meaning. It is only after the experience, whether immediately following, or with a delay, that the subject might begin exhausting the possible meanings underlying this emotion, in order to uncover the actual cause(s) beneath his uncontrollable feelings. At least, this is what we observe over the course of analysis; both analysand and analyst. These feelings are perceived as both psychical and bodily experiences. However, what is most real about the experience of such feelings is the feelings themselves. They are deceptive; might be in disguise, transformed or displaced, but are always signalling towards something real and significant, underneath. Hence, in the clinic, tracing these feelings back can lead to an understanding of key components of unconscious thoughts (signifiers), fantasies (which support the subject's desire), Freudian familial drama, or Lacanian personal myth or the drive. We can hide our feelings from others around us, but we are not able to block them from being expressed or perceived. They always have their ways of surprising us. According to both Freud and Lacan, feelings themselves are not repressed; they indicate a repressed signifier. In other words, feelings, as manifestations of affects, and what they represent are linked in the unconscious; while what is felt is conscious. In spite of a trendy approach in the treatment of unpleasant feelings, which emphasises the advice: "Don't shy away" from experiencing, expressing or sharing them with others, feelings are not treatable. On the other hand, dismissing and normalising bad feelings by blaming them on current culture and social discourse also prevents us from understanding the unthinkable, causative factors that generate these feelings. Essentially, we cannot stop ourselves or others from experiencing unexpected feelings, no matter how long we have spent on trying to understand them at root. This is the reason why the work of analysis is not simply focused on getting rid of bad feelings: that would be the wrong focus – feelings are disingenuous, and keep returning to surprise the subject. This attitude does not, of course, exclude examination of feelings (as experienced affects) from the psychoanalytic clinic. But giving credence only to how a subject should or should not feel diverts the clinic away from exploring what constitutes the unconscious. Moreover, if the analysis of the symptom (which acts only as the translator of jouissance into the Real) is meant to offer a solution to the subject after destitution, there must be a price. Feelings, as they are also markers from the Real, remind the subject what is done to the symptom during analysis. In other words, it is impossible for the subject to have agency over forming a new way of being, before being ready to challenge his unconscious knowledge. Affects are where the subject's central certainties and beliefs are challenged. This is particularly true of the experience of anguish; an affect which was considered non-deceptive by Lacan. In analysis, every subject has to comb back through memories from their past, with definite consequences on his emotional state. In most cases of difficult feelings, we are bereaved by losing our unconscious fantasies (which results in grief); we can become terribly anxious when reminded of our subjective division or when our symptom fails to index the painful Real for us (which causes anguish); we might even feel numb – not comfortably, though! – in a sort of bodily deadness or frozen mind; or we might suffer from a bruised ego (annoyance or anger), swear to never look back again, and yet still keep going back. Despite all the different sorts of feelings we might go through, we endure the pain, we endorse all sorts of unpleasant feelings, hoping to finally break free from the suffering induced by our mode of being. These ups and downs, swinging from one different feeling to the next, are inevitable. There is no hiding from the past; from the Other of language and its marks on our Real body. We might have ended up in analysis in order to treat an overwhelming suffering that was initially felt as an affect, such as anxiety attacks or deep sadness. Psychoanalysis does not offer an effective treatment to these affects, but, by focusing on the pain of the Real, helps a subject to regain agency and the ability to rearrange their indexing of the Real. Therefore, analysis is not the first step in the clinical treatment of a suffering subject who is overwhelmed with distressing feelings. He is in a mute, dark pain: all he is after is recovery, and never to go through that experience again. Such a state of feeling – to the extent of being in pain – is indeed different from experiencing this while in analysis.

For Freud, feelings were the manifestation of affects, and affects were the expression of the drive (Freud, 1925–6). The drive, is silent in the language, but certainly not in the body. One example from Lacan's teaching on affects is the expression of the scopic drive in the form of shame. In the clinic, the role of the gaze, as the object of the scopic drive, is always present, throughout the process of tracing back shame.

Another affect that can be associated with the scopic drive is "fear" – as fright. Fright is another unpleasant feeling that can rise up to haunt the subject when a potential threat to his subjective existence is present. The fear of losing the gaze, or fear of an empty gaze – like a pair of black holes looking at the subject. Fearing for one's life, sanity or physical health can be felt as a bodily excitation. It can range from a tickle to a blaze of anguish, as Lacan tells us in his 17th seminar, when describing the state of jouissance (Lacan, 1969–70). Fear resulting in avoidance can also be understood through Freud's work on obsessional neurosis and the anal drive; while disgust in hysteria is linked to the oral drive.

Among all the aforementioned affects, there is one privileged affect which can often be misunderstood when placed alongside other psychical perceptions or be mis-presented in the clinic: anguish. It is privileged because, according to Lacan, it does not lie and can be the guiding light in the clinic. It is the ultimate form of all other affects. There are other ways of being unsettled which are also commonly referred to as "anguish" in everyday life, or even in a clinical setting: stress, distress, panic, temptation, fear, excitation. However, the anguish is a pure agony which haunts the subject at the bodily level and is experienced rather than being properly described in the subject's narratives. It is not a playful game of excitation, nor is it what we might experience in relation to the Other's demand. It is outside language – outside meaning and structure. It is an unthinkable sensation that descends upon the subject whose own perspective and knowledge fail to save him, in the moment of experience. A variety of different subjects of all kinds of psychical structures have testified to their experience of it, in clinic and in the literature of psychoanalysis. In the moment, the subject just wants to be saved from it. In such anguish, the body's reactions attest to such an overwhelming force, to the extent that many try to find its cause in a possible physical illness. It is somewhat accurate to think of a physical illness or a slowly mortifying body as a cause responsible for the experience of anguish. This metaphor might raise underlying questions around a subject's mode of being; in relation to his symptom, his desire or the drive. After all, the symptom (which acts to index the Real) does not exist outside the Real body. In this respect, we could also wonder about Lacan's concept of anguish as an affect, and his work on jouissance as a bodily excitation. Lacan's later works on the symptom, the Real and jouissance do not exclude affects, and particularly not anguish. The anguish experienced as part of the analytical process and the anguish brought to analysis to be treated, can guide the clinic; unlike all other affects, which are not allies to the analyst's attempts to interpret. One has to endure the pain of anguish as a part of subjective destitution, in order to evolve into a new subject whose sinthome is formed after his symptom is butchered.

Once, in a session with an analysand who was discussing and rationalising her relationship with one of her family members, the analysand suddenly stopped talking and started shaking on the couch. She got up and asked for help: "My panic's back. I can't let this happen again", she said. A couple of minutes later, once she had been somewhat calmed down, she left. The meeting had, out of nowhere, turned into a distressing situation. In a few hours' time, after checking in on her condition, she replied by sending an extract from a poem. It was a relief to receive those lines of poetry: she had found a way to describe the agony which was in evidence all over her body. Over subsequent weeks, she went through a difficult time with her anguish, before she was able to face analysis again. She came back when she was ready to talk. It is impossible for anyone to even imagine exactly what she was going through – I had experienced the anguish myself, many years earlier, and I knew I had to wait for her. She had initially come for analysis for the anxiety attacks that started soon after her marriage. Over the course of analysis, she had many times attempted to investigate the different contexts in which she had felt anxious – naming these experiences as being all the same. However, this was the first occasion in a long time that she had again re-experienced what had brought her into analysis in the first place. At the beginning of treatment, she was still on anti-anxiety medication, until eventually she was ready to become an analysand. The most recent episode of panic had shocked her and she was wary of re-experiencing it; however, despite her fear of going through the experience again, she was able to question her way of being (as a desiring subject) just after this incident. What she had experienced from the Real, had momentarily shaken her to the core of her being. No words, but rather the fragment of a poem that had a historical significance for her, was what could be shared with the Other, while giving a clue towards the reason for her suffering. The unthinkable, had slipped through, from outside of the subject's control, and found a means to be expressed. Her anguish – described and felt as a "blaze" – was like no other emotional state or anxiety. She was spooked, yet with no apparent existing fear to alarm her. The work of analysis on her symptom at last became possible only further to such a disturbing, haunting experience. The mark of a much earlier loss had caused her to grieve for most of her life. Her grief over "what" was missing in her love object was the question to be taken on board.

Feelings – as "discourse without speech" – (Lacan, 1969–70) are the expressions of a repressed thought. Therefore, they are markers of an unconscious truth. Not all feelings and emotions are the allies of analytical interpretation. The affects, which are given space in analysis, are not the same as daily annoyance and anger, dissatisfaction and frustration or intermittent low mood or stress. The principal affects discussed in theories of Lacanian psychoanalysis are: rage and hatred in sexual envy, ignorance, boredom and morosity following realisation of the sexual non-rapport, guilt as a sort of wrongdoing to the Other or as a result of over-enjoyment, shame when exposed to the object of the scopic drive, gaiety and enthusiasm upon discovering of an unconscious knowledge, grief and mourning after loss of an unconscious phantasy and the anguish that arises when the subject is engulfed by an opaque jouissance. In the analytical setting – as Lacan tells us – anguish is the one emotion of all those that a subject might experience in daily life which does not deceive. The pain of encounter with the sexual non-rapport is expressed in extreme anxiety and fear (fright). But such affects are really an expression of cowardice: *wanting to know nothing* about the sexual non-rapport (Soler, 2016). When a subject is faced with the question of his or her sexuality as a social being, an unpleasant feeling is generated. The question to work through in the clinic is that of the context, in which a subject has been faced with this unbearable Real of sexuality. It is then up to the subject to take his own particular path to the question of his or her sexuality and somehow overcome this "cowardice" regarding the fact of the sexual non-rapport. It is only after enduring the attendant pain that a less unsettling and disturbing defence against the Real of sexuality can be constructed.

The sexual non-rapport and feelings in the culture of modern Iran

I would like to conclude with a vignette – a personal experience of the emotions, which have been described, based on three scenes from my own childhood. Through this vignette we will refer to the psychoanalytical approach to the emotions, linked to the subject's experience of the sexual non-rapport, where the creation of a personal myth can (to some extent) make up for the sexual non-rapport. Do we not, in the course of an analysis, move away from the narratives of myths and the deceptive emotions attached to them towards the realisation of the sexual non-rapport?

There is a semi-humorous, contemporary Iranian anecdote about the definition of a "perfect" woman. The perfect woman is one who can successfully manage three areas of her life: family (the kitchen), profession (the office) and sex (the bedroom). A "wise" woman keeps the three areas as separate as possible while taking pride in being skilful in each of them. A foolish woman confuses the three areas: she bosses people around in the kitchen, seduces colleagues at the office and smells like a cook in the bedroom.

From a psychoanalytic perspective, a subject's ethics play a significant role in choosing his/her mode of life. Ethics in analysis is certainly not the same as rationality. Between the Symbolic dimension of culture – to which we are born – and the Imaginary dimension of education and upbringing (learning social life skills), our unconscious interprets the Real jouissance of the Other in order to find a meaning for our sexed being (phallic signification) in language to form a symptom, which is supported by the scenario of a fantasy. When a subject is cornered between the jouissance of the Other and his desire, a course of action is chosen, based on that subject's ethical stance.

And so, to the childhood vignette. During a single month one summer, as a young child, I encountered three scenes, all involving a version of womanhood in three different women, each of whom presented their subjective stance between the incongruity of jouissance (of their being) and the cultural discourse in which their stance was perceived and judged. In other words, each of the women approached the sexual non-rapport in her individual way.

In each of the three encounters I was cast in the role of observer or spectator. The position of the spectator, in a theatrical sense, has played a key role in theorisation of the emotions from the ancient world to the formation of psychoanalysis (the construction in Freudian family drama or reduction in Lacanian personal myth). Freud's reference to the Oedipal myth (best known though Sophocles' drama) as well as the stage of his Irma dream are not to be approached and evaluated simply as enactments of emotional states (the cathartic approach), but rather as a way of taking the question of sexuality on board. It is from the stage of the Freudian family drama that an individual fashion a "personal myth" (in Lacan's expression) that allows him or her to come to terms with the tragedy of the sexual non-rapport.

It was the last summer before I started primary school. My aunt, a free spirit with frank and witty humour, was accompanying me and my sister to my parents, who would take us to the countryside, where we spent each summer. On the way to my parents, I saw a crowd of people circling around a woman who had been convicted of a crime. Through a gap in the crowd I saw her on the ground and a male and a female guard standing by her. A woman next to my aunt said: "She was caught with two men in her flat. Her neighbours complained to the authorities that she had turned her flat into a brothel". I saw from the movements of my aunt's hands that the scene makes her upset and nervous, but she kept calm and tried to calm me by speaking light-heartedly: "Oh darling, she was a greedy, you can cover up for one but two gets you into trouble. It's bound to!" However, the anxiety aroused in me by the image of the fallen woman was not dissipated. The woman was exposed to the accusatory gaze of a crowd because of an assumed wrong doing. My anger towards such violence was expressed few minutes later in a tantrum and a fight with my little sister.

I spent the next few days depressed. About a week later, I was playing with an old and grumpy turtle in the garden (trying to feed him) when I caught a burst of song, coming from the dark room at the end of the garden. A chorus of women's voices was singing a folk song against the background sound of a hammer striking a soft surface, like percussion. Without understanding the song, I was immediately fascinated by the sound and rhythm coming from inside the room. But by the time I reached the door, both rhythm and chant had stopped. The women were skilled artisans knotting a silk Persian rug. I saw a half-finished rug in colourful silks hung in front of the women, who were using a special knife held in one hand to knot the rug with a skill that seemed to me like magic, their hands moving through the threads at superhuman speed. Knot by knot, they were creating a masterpiece. Suddenly, one woman started a new chant and they divided again into two groups: one singing a call and the other replying. The sun's rays fell from a little window in the ceiling onto the floor of the room. The smell of silk fabric and of roses gave a special flavour to the whole experience. A kindly looking, mature woman, who seemed to be supervising the others, invited me inside with open arms. The soft, slow rhythm of their voices was in contrast with their fast-moving, expert hands switching between threads and ties, and wielding the sharp blade. The kindly woman began singing an old folk song of longing, sorrow and love. It was a Persian elegy expressing emotions and feelings, where the death and martyrdom of a loved one is praised, respected and mourned. My anxious gaze fixed on the movements of their hands while the voice of the older woman pacified me. My anxiety over the fetish object of aggression/violence (the action of the sharp knife) was dissipated by the pacifying effect of their chanting and the whole scene of this group of women seemed an expression of real independence and freedom. They were engrossed in their work and deriving pleasure from it.

The same summer concluded with a final evening feast before our return to the city. Relatives and friends of our family, many of whom I never saw again, came together to mark the end of summer (another tradition of unknown origin). Many of the young parents who gathered had professional lives in addition to raising a family. In the garden, I overheard a heated conversion between two women, two reputable architects, each with a drink in her hand and smoking. One of them suddenly turned to me and said: "Enjoy your freedom, little chipmunk! School, work and family life, and then from your forties you retire!" The women looked at each other and burst out laughing. I was attracted by the image of these cool, architect-women, wearing trousers, smoking and drinking whisky. They seemed to me to be free, but apparently, they did not feel the same! I knew of their problematic relationships with their partners, but the discontent with their professional and personal life, expressed in their conversation, did not make the image they projected any less attractive. Later, they both went through acrimonious divorces. They were known as highly successful women outdoors, but were certainly dissatisfied and ill-tempered indoors. Their control over their emotions and endurance of hardship at work were always praised. They were Stoic women!

Later in my own analysis, I discovered that the ethos of my experience in that summer had become the fabric of my personal myth of a feminine position. The agency of the fallen woman and of the two professional women in challenging imposed expectations around the image of the perfect female had been noticed and their access to the Other jouissance ("Autre Jouissance", something I had intuited in the singing artisan women) had marked my weaving of a sinthome.

Bibliography

Freud, S. (1925–6). Inhibition, symptom and anxiety. In: J. Strachey, ed., *The standard edition of the complete psychological works of Sigmund Freud, vol. XX*. London: Vintage, 2001, pp. 77–174.

Lacan, J. (1969–70). *The seminar of Jacque Lacan: Book XVII: The other side of psychoanalysis*. Russell Grigg (Trans.). London: Norton.

Soler, C. (2016). *Lacanian affects: The function of affects in Lacan's work*. B. Fink (Trans.). London and New York: Routledge.

Index